The Fighting Art of

TANG SOO DO

By Darnell Garcia

DISCLAIMER

Please note that the Publisher of this instructional book is NOT RESPONSIBLE in any manner whatsoever for any injury which may occur by reading and/or following the instructions herein.

It is essential that before following any of the activities, physical or otherwise, herein described, the reader or readers should first consult his or her physician for advice on whether or not the reader or readers should embard on the physical activity described herein. Since the physical activities described herein may be too sophisticated in nature, *it is essential that a physician be consulted.*

4201 VANOWEN PLACE, BURBANK, CA 91505

Printed in the United States of America

ISBN: 0-86568-014-0
Library of Congress No.: 81-70816

34567890□86 85 84

Design and Layout by Jeff Dungfelder

Editor: Daniel M. Furuya

Preface

This text describes the art of Tang Soo Do in a very unique way. While it delves into many of the traditional methods, it also intertwines modified concepts and principles apropos to our present day environment. These innovative additions did not come about by accident, but rather through devoted scrutiny triggered by participation in *open tournaments* throughout the world. To be more explicit, this book is unique because the author, Darnell Garcia, is unique. As a contestant, he welcomed every challenge no matter who attended or what styles sponsored the tournaments. His personality, and positive attitude, gained him many friends who were also notable competitors. As these acquaintances blossomed into friendships, brainstorming and analytical comparisons became a common practice. Ironically, competition became a stimulus to co-operation where these practitioners *cared for* as well as *shared with* one another.

You would have to personally see Mr. Garcia in action to appreciate Tang Soo Do as he has refined it. As a devoted advocate who pursued technical avenues, mastery of his movements have unquestionably progressed to higher levels of sophistication. It is this sophistication, along with the basic rudiments of the art, that Mr. Garcia wishes to share with you in his book. He feels that sharing his experiences will lead you to accelerated levels of progress. Having personally explored and experimented with many of the rudiments of the art himself, makes it possible for you to devote more time to strengthen other areas needing consideration.

Darnell Garcia holds many Grand Champion titles. Earning these titles took self-discipline and hard work. Follow his blueprint of success described in his book and become a champion yourself. Are you willing to take up the challenge? Success is yours for the taking. Diligently study this book and your efforts will be rewarded.

Ed Parker

The Author

Born in New York City, raised in Los Angeles, California, a graduate of Los Angeles City College and California State University in Los Angeles, Darnell Garcia was introduced to karate over ten years ago when he attended the 1968 International Karate Championships in Long Beach, California. The next day he visited a Chuck Norris Studio and signed up for a three year course with a dream that one day he too would become the International Champion. It became immediately apparent that he was truly a champion. Considered a gentleman's fighter, he soon won over fifty national tournaments, i.e. Western States Grand Champion, U.S. National Grand Champion, and Top Ten Karate's Fighter Grand Champion. He toured Europe and Hawaii with various teams representing the United States. Then, after four years of long, hard training, in 1972, his dream came true in Long Beach, California when he defeated the legendary Joe Lewis with several crushing blows to the mid-section and became the International Grand Champion. Other karate professionals who have taken second place in competition with Darnell Garcia include Al Dacascos, Byung Yu, Benny Urquidez, Jeff Smith, Bill Owens, Fred Wren, John Natividad, Howard Jackson, Robert Haliburton and numerous other top rated fighters.

Between 1971 and 1975, Darnell taught over 3,000 students and they couldn't have had a better teacher with his record of outstanding achievements. However, shortly thereafter, he retired from active competition and teaching and currently devotes his time to writing and the film industry. *Karate: Explosive Instincts and Mind Power* was his first book of several volumes that he will share with readers on how to maintain a winning edge.

He has appeared in numerous martial arts film classics such as *Enter the Dragon*, *Black Belt Jones*, *Death Force*, *Mr. Means*, *Tiger's Revenge*, *Blind Rage* and *Enforcer from Death Row*, starring Cameron Mitchell and Leo Fong. He is also Vice-President of Production Coordination for Koinonia Films, Inc. who produced such films as *Blind Rage*, *Tiger's Revenge*, *Bamboo Trap*, and *Last Reunion*. In 1981, he was appointed as Vice-President of Borden Films Inc., International Film Distribution.

You may ask, how does one become such a Champion?

The first thing in any endeavor is to have a goal in mind. Without a purpose, one will end up just drifting to nowhere. Although the aspiration to be world champion was a big dream, he felt strongly that one must have the will power to learn and not give up. Karate is more than just physical and technical training, it is also mental. Everyone possesses a vast amount of mind power. Unfortunately, very few have been able to tap and utilize this tremendous resource. One of the implications of mind power is the ability of what one wants to accomplish, then set out to reach those goals, and not settle for anything less. His reputation as a fighter was that of being cool and calculating, making every movement count. Although not always the case inwardly, he had to discipline himself to control his fear and anger. More than that, it was his ability to design a plan and, with self discipline, stay with it.

Hopefully, this book will help you find a goal and develop a plan for success. This is one man's experience in ascending to the top. He did it with a plan. Perhaps, when you discover your goal, you will also realize your plan. If this book aids you in that search or journey to the top, his efforts will have been worth it. Take it from a true Champion and Master of the Arts, Darnell Garcia, a legend in his own time . . . .

Acknowedgements

I wish to take this opportunity to thank Mr. Terry Updike for his help in the area of the Hyungs (forms) and technical editing, Mr. Stuart Farber for his patience with the one-step punching section, Mr. George Dolby for his assistance with the kicking techniques, Ms. Carol Stabler for the self-defense section and Mr. David King for supplying his photographic skills necessary for the materilization of this book.

This book would not have been possible without the vision and support of Mr. Curtis Wong, publisher, and his staff at Unique Publications.

My sincere thanks go to Ms. Eva Sara Halbreich for her time in editing the original manuscript.

And last but not least, my thanks to Mr. Rudy Bareng and Mr. John Jackson.

Foreword

I have known Darnell Garcia for many years and have followed his career from the start. I was there the night he fought the legendary Joe Lewis and took the title away as the reigning champion for Ed Parker's International Tournament. Darnell's precise techniques and calm fighting style beat out one of the top technicians in the art. From that point on, Darnell's career just kept soaring to higher goals.

The techniques Darnell used in his fighting career were from the Tang Soo Do System of Korean Karate. A style that stresses more kicking techniques than hand attacks. This book contains the basic aspects of this fine art and I highly recommend this book for all interested martial art practioners. It doesn't matter what style you practice but how you pursue the best techniques to fit your fighting style. A book is a catalog of training methods and teaching aids to learn about various styles, but a good instructor is still necessary to develop the true essence of the martial arts spirit.

This book will give you insight in seeking out a good instructor that can help you to develop your inner spirit and body. No style is better than another because all the arts are seeking the same goal. The development of the mind, the inner drive of the spirit and the total control of the body should be the goal of each martial artist.

Sifu Douglas Lim Wong
Sil Lum Kung Fu Studio
White Lotus Kung Fu Association

TABLE OF CONTENTS

Introduction

This book is designed for the beginner and intermediate student desiring to pursue or enhance his knowledge of the art of Tang Soo Do. Inasmuch as there has been little written on this subject, I felt compelled to write this book detailing my experiences in Tang Soo Do.

I implore all instructors, regardless of their system or style, to not only teach their students to kick and punch, but also to read and absorb what has been written in this book. To students of other systems or styles, I implore you to make a conscientious effort to obtain the depth of my text. To the critic, I humbly request that I be judged without discrimination. As Shakespeare wrote, "There are more things in heaven and earth than are dreamed of in your philosophy."

This book will hopefully be a vehicle of continued knowledge — a means, not an end. Use it to fulfill your aspirations in the martial arts as it aids you in developing your full potential. I sincerely hope that my efforts will supply you with answers to many of your unanswered questions. As to those questions that will inevitably arise, deeper study will provide you with solutions.

It is also my fervent hope that this book will become a real learning experience for you and that it will stimulate a perpetual desire within you for continued growth in the martial arts. Please allow my book on Tang Soo Do to be an important step in further developing your potential.

What Is Tang Soo Do?

Tang Soo Do is an organized idea, reduced to a physical expression. It is thought refined into action. Moreover, it is a way of self-examination and achievement

Master Hwang Kee, the founder of Tang Soo Do, began this system in 1945, after studying and mastering many forms of martial arts such as the traditional Soo Bank Do. Hwang Kee studied for a time in Northern China where he was exposed to the Tang method of martial arts. Tang Soo Do is an evolution of the Tang method under the inspiration of Hwang Kee in Korea. Hwang Kee presently heads the Moo Duk Kwan Tang Soo Do, a worldwide organization.

If you were to divide modern Tang Soo Do of today into its major influences; in my opinion, sixty percent is Korean, thirty percent is Northern Chinese (soft style) and ten percent is American. I feel that the American influence in classical Tang Soo Do has been tremendous due to the differences in physical make-up of its practitioners here in America (as opposed to Korea) and also due to the differences in environment and attitudes.

Tang Soo Do in America is becoming more prolific due to the efforts of notable Tang Soo Do practitioners such as Chuck Norris, Terry Upkide and John Natividad. Undoubtedly, the single most influential instructor thus far, in shaping the development of Tang Soo Do in America today, would be Chuck Norris. Norris currently has over three hundred black belts trained under him. He began his schools in the traditional Tang Soo Do method but he has gradually evolved in his personal style of martial arts and his influence has been no less than significant.

Master Hwang Kee's son is currently coordinating the promotional aspects as well as individual studio participation into a national organization of Tang Soo Do in America. Various schools such as the Torrance Tang Soo Do Karate Studio of which Terry Updike is the Chief Instructor, are continuing to enhance, develop and carry on the fundamental tradition of this art.

Fifteen years ago, there were only several hundred practitioners of Tang Soo Do. Today, I would venture to say that there are more than 7500 practitioners on the West Coast alone, and approximately 20,000 throughout the world.

Attitudes In Training

The student should not forget that whether it is Tang Soo Do or any other form of martial art, all martial arts share basically the same historical evolution. At some point in time, when primitive man had to defend himself against his enemies, martial arts were born. When you have no weapon, you must become a weapon yourself.

The student beginning Tang Soo Do must understand clearly what he is studying and the purpose of his training. A martial art is basically an art of warfare and personal self-defense. It has many benefits and by-products outside of this scope. One is self-confidence and the other is improved health and well-being through physical exercise and training. The one single element required to achieve this, however, is discipline.

To begin your training with an attitude that you must either win or inevitably lose a fight is futile. In one of my prior publications, "Explosive Instincts and Mind Power," I devoted the entire book to discussing the proper attitude towards training for the beginning student.

There are six stages of development involved in cultivating the correct attitude towards the art of Tang Soo Do and its concept of training. A beginner should endeavor to develop the proper frame of mind before starting Tang Soo Do or any martial arts career.

Consciousness is the first stage. Consciousness, simply put, is being aware of what is available. For instance, you cannot begin correct training in Tang Soo Do without a qualified instructor. It is impossible to learn the fundamental principles of focus, power and inner strength without proper guidance and supervision. By picking up this book and coming to understand what it has to say, you have taken one step towards consciousness, as you are now aware of what is available in the many aspects of the art of Tang Soo Do.

Goal Setting, the second stage of developing an appropriate attitude, is very important in life which includes your career, work, aspirations, and the aims you hope to achieve. Whatever kind of work you do, you must say to yourself, "I am at this point today, with patience and effort in two or three years, I will come to this point in my life or I will have achieved this level in my aspirations." Without goal setting, you will never have the ability to gauge your progress and evaluate your areas of weakness. Without a conscious effort to set goals and determine your progress, you may perhaps, through inattentiveness and negligence, remain in the same starting position all your life. In Tang Soo Do training, you may begin as a white belt and plan your training to accomplish a green belt within a given time period continually setting up short range goals for yourself. Setting goals, whether they be long or short range, is an important aspect in gauging progress and determining levels of skill in your training.

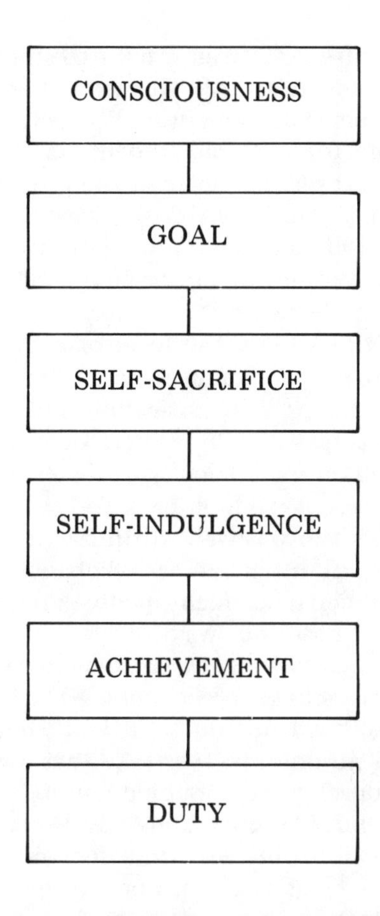

In mentioning the color belt system, although belt ranks help you set up goals, the belt itself means nothing more than a convenient method to hold up your pants, whether you are a white, green or black belt. You are the result of your training, experience and the goals that you have set for yourself in the art of Tang Soo Do. You are not the belt; the belt only marks time in relation to others not yourself. People who brag about their ranks and have an exaggerated veneration for the belt system place too much confidence in things which stand outside of themselves. This is an indication of a serious lack of self-confidence and self-understanding. The belt only has meaning when it truly represents the skill and level of its owner. But a belt is still a belt, and sometimes, it is more important to hold up your pants than your pride.

The third stage of your mental development is *self-sacrifice.* This is important because of what it asks of you and what it demands of you. What will you have to give up to acquire knowledge in Tang Soo Do? The complaint I hear most often is, "Well, I want to study the martial arts, but I don't have the time to devote to it." This excuse is one given by those who are already poor achievers. You can always recognize success by the sacrifice made and the price paid for it. Some students say they can't learn because they don't have the proper place to train or the proper uniform. These are all excuses not to do what you, deep down inside, want and need to do. Abraham Lincoln first studied in a humble cabin without the advantages of a Harvard Law School education. In the beginning of his career, Chuck Norris studied and trained his students in his own backyard.

Self sacrifice many times takes the form of enduring physical pain. You finish a hard day at work and when it comes time for training, you find that it is difficult to find the proper motivation and energy. You must push yourself a little harder to get a little farther. There can be no gain without a little pain. Do not dwell on the difficulty of the effort or training, just do it. After a time, you will be able to look back and see the progress and see that the additional effort and pain was well worth it.

Self-Indulgence is the fourth stage and probably the most deceptive and the most difficult to understand. Many people are afraid of self-indulgence primarily because they have no way of controlling it. After you have achieved a desired level, you owe yourself some reward. For instance, having trained for a number of years and reaching the black belt status, you should now be able to work out when you want and where you want. You have earned your status and no one can ever take that away from you. Now you are in the position to develop new training methods for yourself. "*Nothing ever remains the same and your art.*" Tang Soo Do requires that you become innovative. You may now, for the first time, seek new training aids since you are no longer a novice. This is the proper perspective of self-indulgence; freedom to make a choice as a by-product of your discipline and training. The major pitfall of this kind of self-indulgence is forgetting where you came from. One problem occurs when a young black belt may start something that already exists. Remember that you may not know all there is to know about your own style. Self-indulgence has some limits. Reach them, expand them, and continue to grow with them.

The next step on the chart of progressiveness is achievement. Achievement takes many forms and may, like beauty, exist only "in the eyes of the beholder". Achievement is your own interpretation. No one else can define it for you. Someone may say, "you won a trophy, what an achievement." But only you know how lucky you may have been to win or how you felt when you won it. Only you can determine whether you were at your best or not. In life as well as in the martial arts, some people reach high levels of achievement early and some never achieve anything. Age does not necessarily merit success. You will be able to understand achievement at a point in your career with Tang Soo Do, but remember, it is a progression with which only you can identify with by yourself. It may be as simple as the perfection of a front kick, as challenging as winning a world championship or as complex as the development of a new aspect in the art of Tang Soo Do.

The last stage of your development is *duty*. After you acquire a substantial level of knowledge, you are bound by duty to pass your knowledge on to new practititioners. You are also expected to help refine the art of Tang Soo Do. This stage of development will show your sincerity and obligation towards the martial arts and the general good that results from its training. At this stage, you will also understand and realize the power you possess over others. The power you have developed is an inner power because of your discipline and an eternal power because of your ability and skill. Your duty will be to use your art only when you have no other choice. You must use only that amount of force necessary to overcome the obstacle that presents itself to you. The force required may be a peaceful compromise or a dynamic flying side kick. Your duty is not only to others but to yourself also. You must always carry on your desire for knowledge and direction.

CHAPTER

ONE

Hand Techniques

This section is on the proper striking methods and the proper usage of the hands. As an illustration and inspiration for the beginning students; Mr. Farber is one of Tang Soo Do's youngest students to achieve a black belt, earning his junior black belt at the early age of ten years old. Nine years later, Mr. Farber has developed into one of Tang Soo Do's most skillful practitioners. In the following photographs, make careful note of the proper hand positions to use in order to avoid unnecessary injury to the hands and bones. When executing the following strikes, pay very close attention to the starting positions.

There are numerous methods of training your hands such as pounding beans, gravel or other hard objects. These types of exercises should only be done under the close supervision of a qualified instructor. This section focuses on the proper forms and the practice of hand and arm positions. The student should try to learn both the English and Korean terms of each position. It is culturally enriching for the student to learn both languages and with closer scrutiny of the original Korean texts, the beginning student will develop a working knowledge of the Korean language.

BASIC FIST

1. Start with open relaxed hand.

2. Slowly close the hand and slowly tighten the fist; the thumb is on outside of fingers.

3. Tense the clutched fist until first two knuckles protrude outwardly.

4. The wrist must be rigid and straight, in a single line from the first two knuckles to the elbow.

The best method for development of a stronger fist is to use a round hard object (pipe, stick) and to curl the object into your hand from twenty to thirty times within one hour keeping in mind to start softly and tense more as you go through repetitions.

Hand Techniques

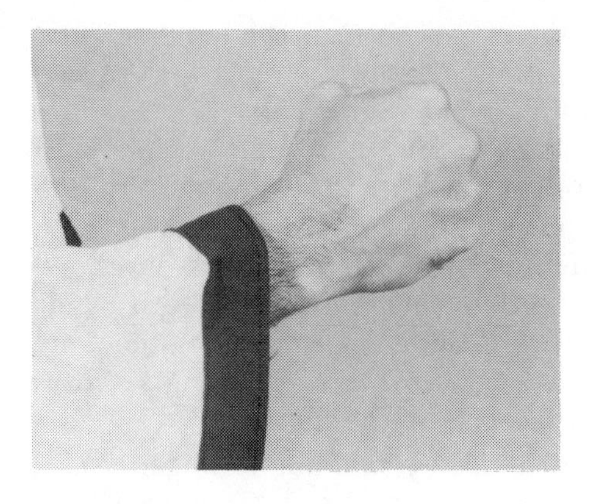

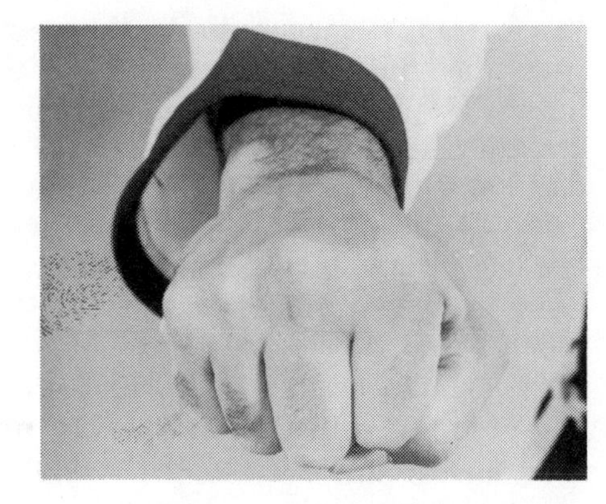

Reverse Punch

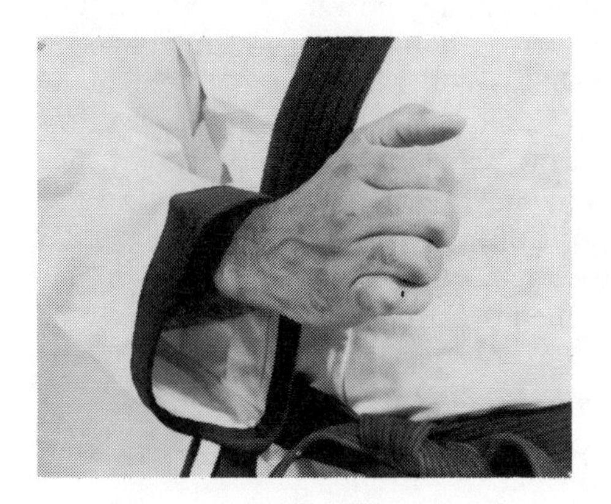

Palm Heel

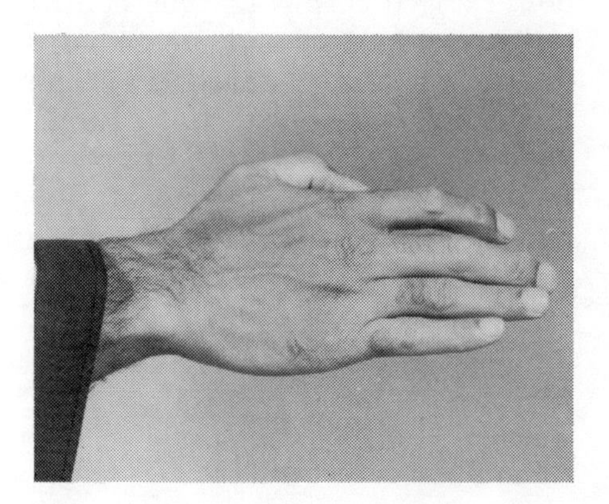

Knife— Hand

After the basic idea of a closed fist is achieved, the next progression is to tie that fist into a strong wrist. As stated earlier in this text, to avoid bone damage or injury, the beginning student is taught to build those areas which require absorbing shock. *"Five for a stronger Five."* Wrist development has many forms, one method which is commonly used in Tang Soo Do Schools is a push-up. (1) Starting with the standard version i.e. the open hand is flat, shoulder width apart and the body is straight from the toes to shoulder. When a beginner can push up at least seventy-five sets, then he is ready for the next phase of wrist development

(2) From the same position the next exercise is to turn the hands inward with the fingers facing each other, elbows at this point are turned outward. Again when seventy-five push-ups can be accomplished, the next phase of development is ready. (3) Starting from a push-up position, turn *one* hand upward so that the body weight rests on the back side of the hand. Again, a set of seventy-five push-ups should be achieved with emphasis of body weight placed on the hand-up side. After this one sided exercise is finished, (4) the hands should be reversed, to build both hands evenly. (5) After seventy-five repetitions are done on each side, the final fifth phase is done by placing both hands upward and executing seventy-five push-ups with the total weight on the back of the hands.

It should also be noted that while push-ups are building stronger wrists, they are developing the next extension of a strong fist which is the shoulder. Shoulder development is not a muscle builder alone, the properly built shoulder is in possession of "braking" power. "Braking power" is that power that controls the stopping power of a punch. For instance, when a hand technique is delivered, it has to have control to be stopped within a fraction of an inch. When this kind of power is developed, "snap" is the natural by-product. One technique to develop "braking power" is by placing the arms straight out in front of the shoulder, directly in front of the body, start with closed fist using the knuckles as a sight guide. From this position, place the body in front of a wall, position the knuckles on the wall and lean away a quarter of an inch. After this position is assumed, punches should be thrown rapidly at the wall without touching the wall. Punches are to be executed with power and speed. This develops "snap, braking power and focus"; all essential in proper punching technique. This is the essence of hand techniques.

Hand Techniques

1. Proper Fist (Juyg Kown)
   a. The proper fist strikes with the first two knuckles. Should be made on a flat plane.

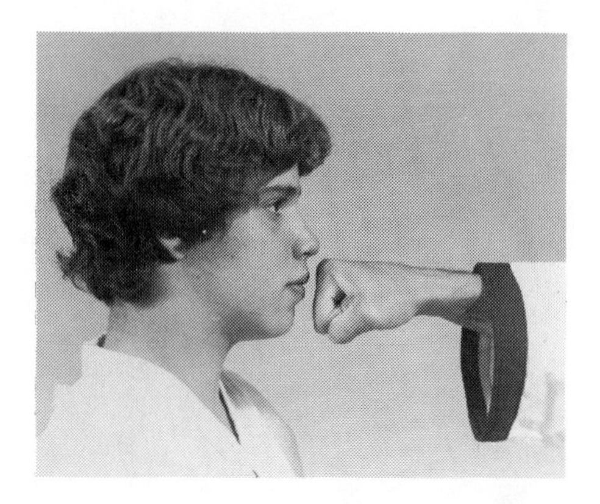

b. Side view of a punch to the face.

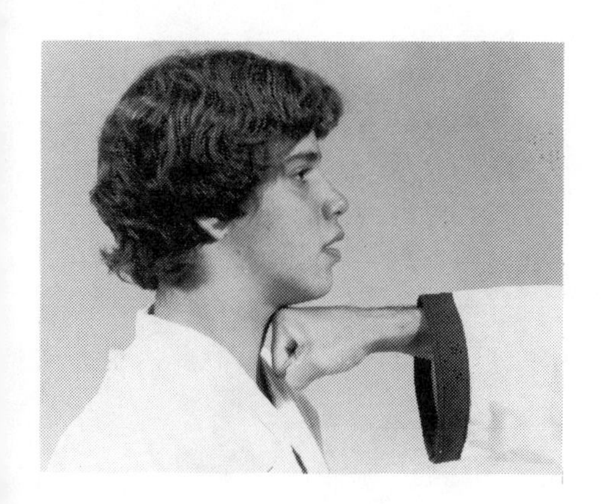

c. Strike to the throat.

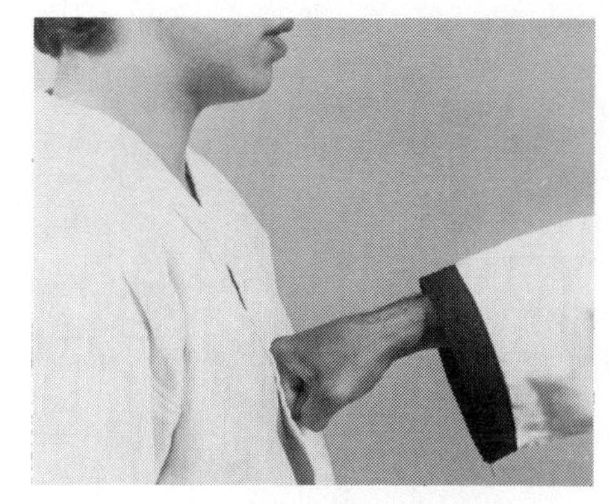

d. Strike to the solar plexis.

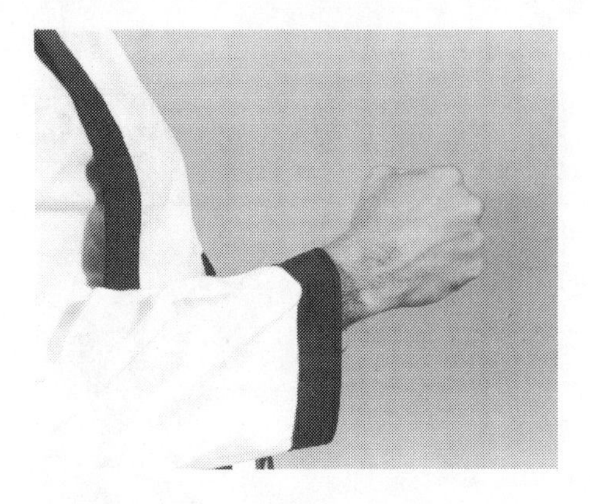

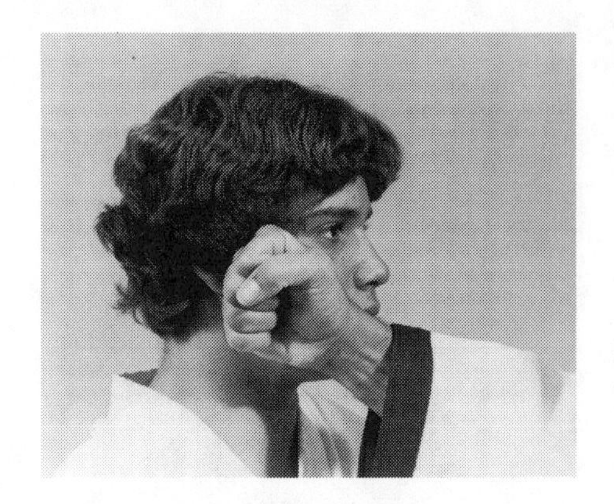

2. Back Fist (Kap Kwon)
   a. The back fist strikes with the first two knuckles on the back of the fist.

b. Back fist to the temple.

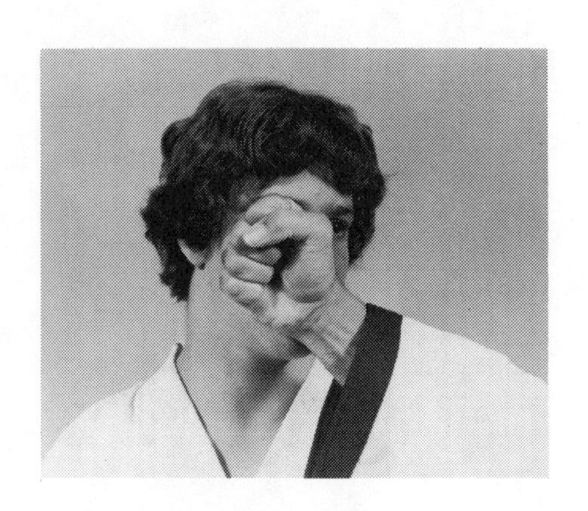

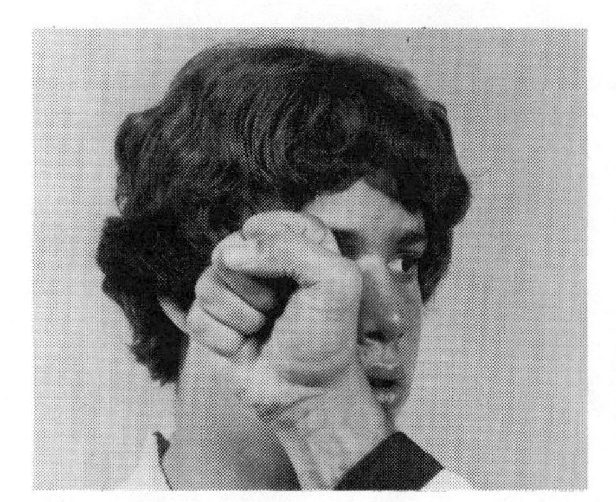

c. Back fist to the face.

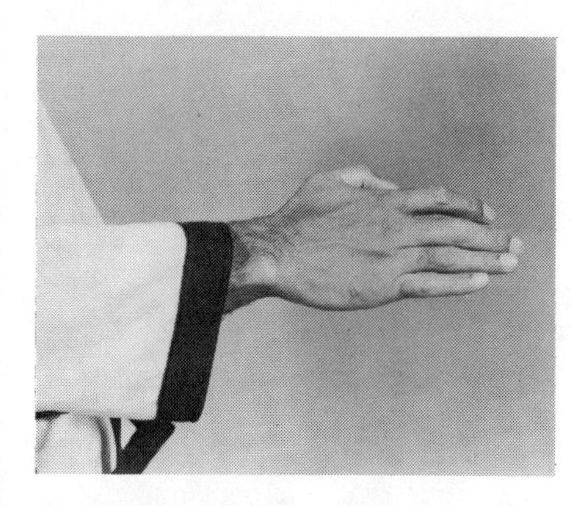

3. Knife Hand Strike (Soo Do)

a. Starting position in the classical stance.

b. Proper hand position for the knife hand strike.

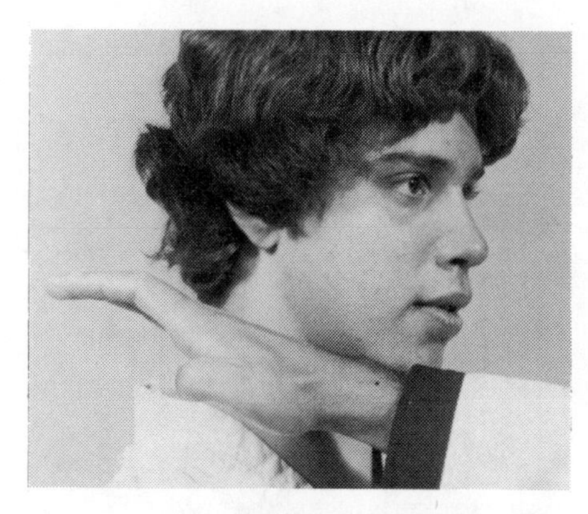

c. Striking to the neck.

4. Reverse Knife Hand (Yuk Soo Do)
   a. Starting position.

b. Proper hand position is also known as the ridge hand strike. The striking area is the inside of the hand.

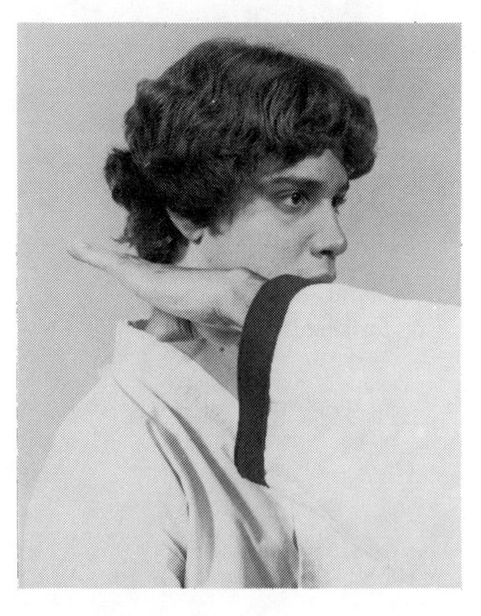

c. Striking the neck.

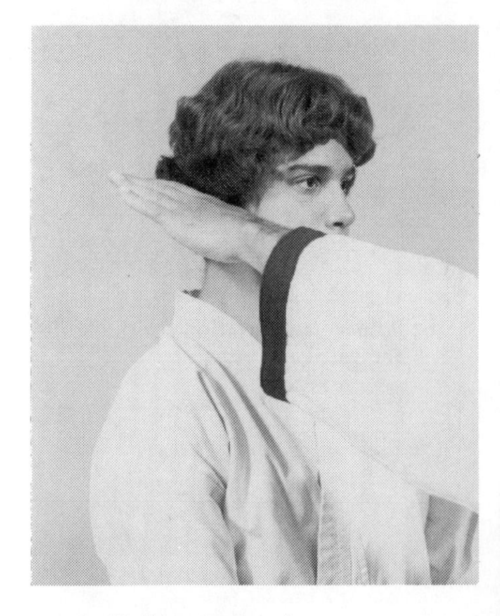

d. Striking the head.

5. Spear Hand (Kwan Soo)

a. Starting position.

b. Spear hand strike.

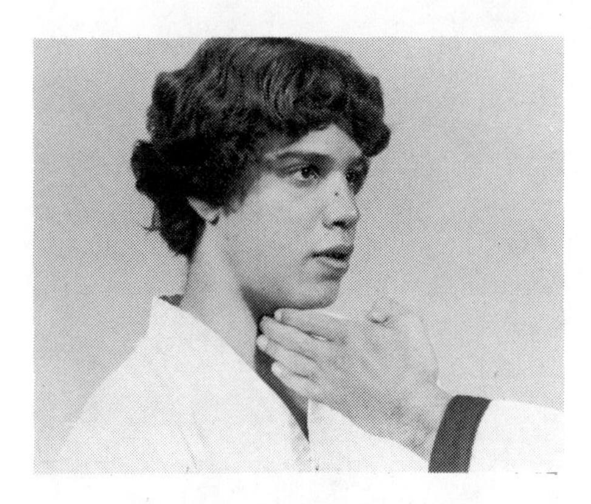

This strike is used like an arrow driving straight into your target with the fingers first.

6. Knuckle Hand (Ban Jul Kwan Soo)

a. Proper hand position.

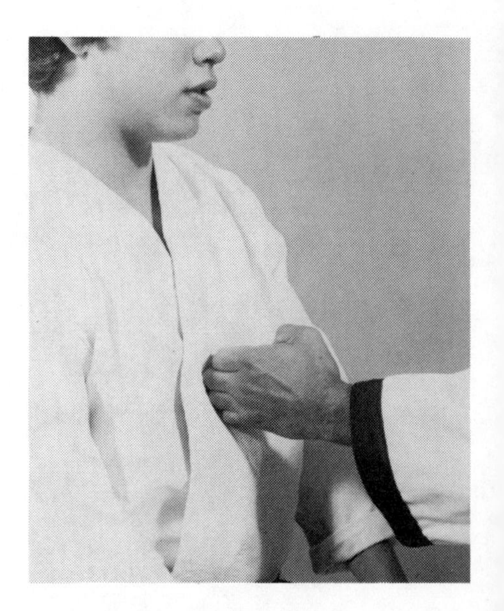

b. Proper strike.
This particular strike is as strong as a fist.

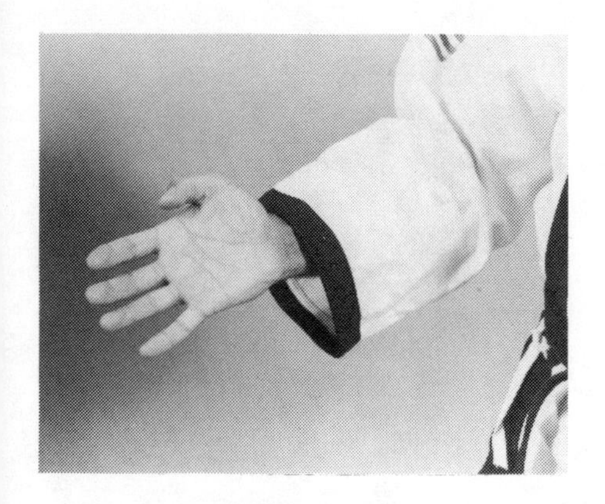

7. Open Hand (Jip Kye Son)

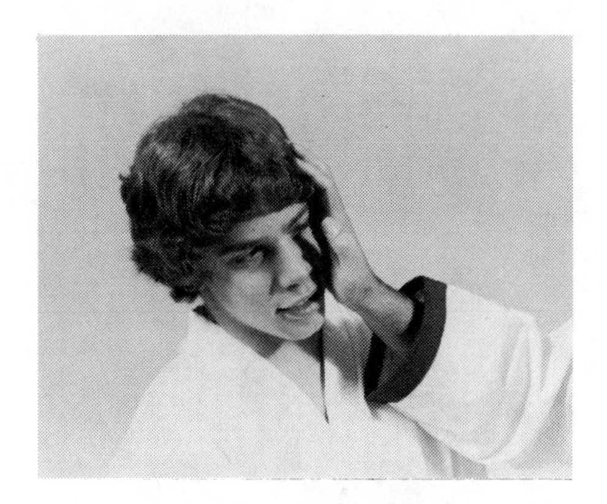

a. Proper position.

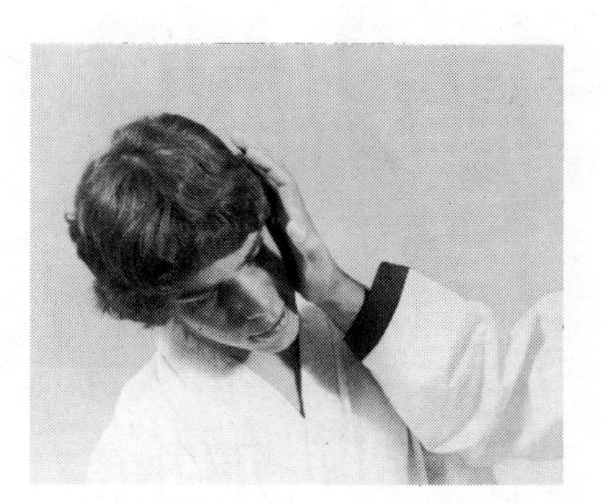

b. Striking.
A slap is commonly used as a weapon, in Tang Soo Do, you use basically the same hand position but begin with the ridge hand position.

8. Palm Hand (Jank Kwon)
   a. Proper hand position.

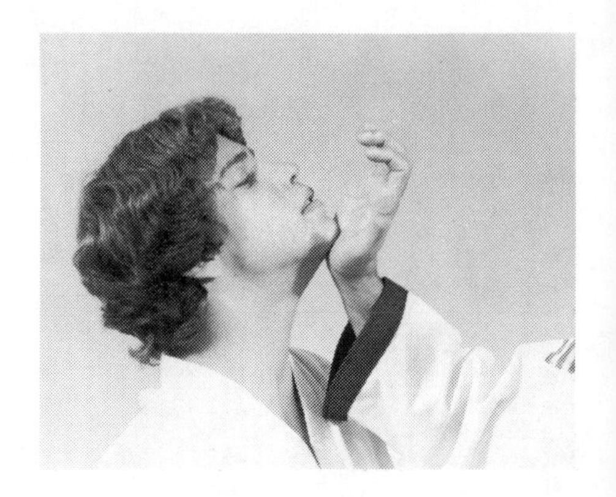

b. Striking with the palm area only. Do not use the fingers in this strike.

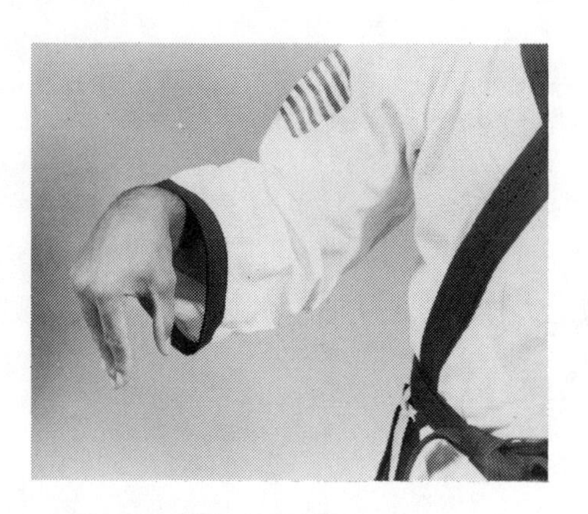

9. Wrist Hand Strike (Pal Mok)
   a. Starting position.

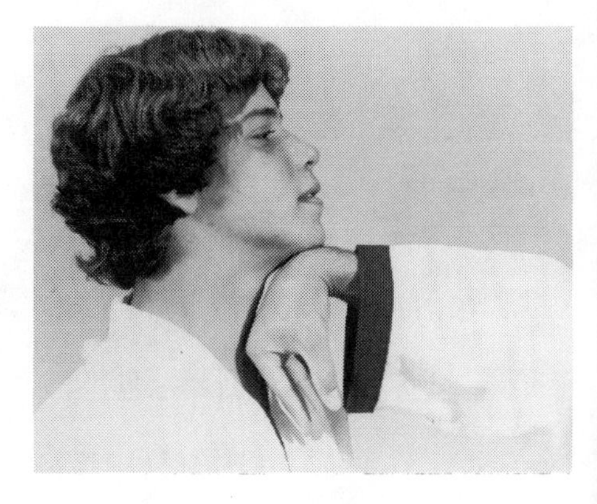

b. Striking.

10. Elbow Strike (Pal Koop)
    a. Striking area.

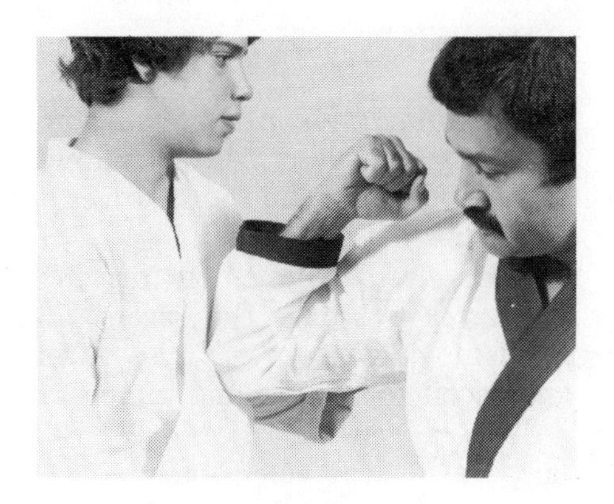

b. Driving with the ball (striking area) of the elbow.

In all of the preceeding strikes, practice is the key to successful execution. It is good advice to perform all of the techniques during the day whenever you have some free time while working or playing. You do not necessarily have to be in the training hall to practice. Practice constantly and continually by assuming the proper hand position and tensing or gripping to strengthen the hand in that position. Good advice is to flex and relax the hand for each position with at least twenty five repetitions per position. Practice one position, rest one hour, then practice another until the entire range of the hand positions have been completed. After a few short months of honest effort and practice, you will notice stronger control of the hands and arms resulting in a stronger, more effective striking force. This is forty percent of Tang Soo Do.

Punching And Striking

REVERSE PUNCH

The foundation of punching in Tang Soo Do is the reverse punch. This punch is best described as follows: Starting with a tight fist from the side of the body, as the fist is driven toward its target, a half twist is executed six inches before impact.

The reverse punch is driven from the hip position of the body. Whenever possible, the reverse punch is delivered by the thrust of one hand moving into the target and the opposite hand drawing back for snap and recoil for the second punch.

It is a general rule to throw a reverse punch at a still target. The purpose is clear when examined closely. This punch has exact focus and a concentrated path, therefore, impact is strongest with the reverse punch.

The same reverse punch is derived from the twisting action of the wrist. Beginning with the idea that all bones and muscles should be utilized to the utmost to achieve maximum power.

The reverse punch is never delivered from a non-balanced position, also a true reverse punch does not allow for over-extension. This punch is "*FORM*" from beginning to end. There is no allowance for poor form or innovation.

In a street fight or tournament competition, the reverse punch is always the most effective for stopping your adversary or scoring point against a competitor. In all the basic Hyung (forms), the reverse punch is found, and is also the first technique used to teach a beginner Hyungs.

SIDE PUNCH

A side punch is delivered from the side of the body just as a reverse punch, but before impact, the entire body is shifted into the punch. The arm is level with shoulder, the body is in line with arm turned sideways.

This punch allows the total use of body weight for power. The snap comes within the last twelve inches before impact.

To examine this punch more closely, we must begin with the starting position before impact. This punch can be delivered from any standing position. A standing position is necessary simply because body weight is important in the thrust of the snap. One half of the body is held back before the final execution of this punch. After the punch is effected, the entire body is turned sideways in a straight line from the fist through the shoulders and again the hip gives a large thrust.

The side punch is first seen by the basic student in Form (Hyung) III where the punch is used three times down the center of the form.

This punch is almost never used in a fighting encounter because of the total commitment that is called for in proper delivery.

BACK FIST

This strike is self-evident using the back of the hand, but striking with the first two knuckles to avoid damage to soft side of the hand.

When properly used, this weapon can be most effective. The limit of this hand technique is that it requires an extension of the arm. While there is power in this technique, one must be aware of some of the hazards in the execution of the strike. One common hazard is over-extending the arm. Sharp pain is the result of a straight (over-extended) elbow when throwing this strike and missing the target. Always keep in mind that a good back-fist requires a bent elbow and loose shoulder. This technique is basically a counter-attack punch or strike.

When an attacker throws punches and kicks and you are able to dodge or block the attack, the smoothest and possibly easiest counter is a back-fist.

Many tournament fighters use this technique simply because it can be controlled early and avoids over-exposure of the body. The main drawback of this technique is, that after a back-fist is thrown as a weapon, the entire body has to re-cock itself back to a forward position.

BOTTOM FIST

One of the strongest portions of the hand and most frequently mis-used. Whenever a person uses his hand to pound a table with a fist, he is using the "bottom of his fist". This is used in Tang Soo Do from the spinning position as in Form III.

THREE STEP PUNCH TECHNIQUE I

1. Starting position. (Farber will deliver three step center punches.)

2. First punch: inside block by Garcia.

3. Second punch: Garcia steps back with another inside block.

4. Third punch: Garcia pivots with another inside block.

5. Garcia strikes with an open hand strike to the face.

6. Garcia grabs Farber and cocks the leg for a sweep.

7. Execution of the sweep.

8. Left hand cocks for a reverse punch.

9. Execution of the reverse punch.

10. Garcia draws the leg to deliver a heel smash.

THREE STEP PUNCH TECHNIQUE II
1. Starting position.

2. First punch by Farber: outside block by Garcia.

3. Second punch: inside block.

4. Third punch: outside block.

5. Open hand smash by Garcia.

6. Follow-up with a center punch.

ONE STEP PUNCHING TECHNIQUE I

1. Starting position. (Garcia is attacking.)

2. Garcia executes a stepping center punch: outside block with the right hand by Dolby.

3. Dolby executes a left hand strike.

4. Dolby continues with a right hand upper punch.

5. Dolby grabs the attacking hand and cocks the foot for a standing round kick.

6. Execution and delivery of the round kick.

ONE STEP PUNCHING TECHNIQUE II

1. Starting position. Dolby attacks Garcia.

2. Dolby executes a stepping center punch: Garcia executes a double high block.

3. Garcia grabs the arm and elbow.

4. Garcia pivots twisting Dolby's arm down at the elbow.

5. Garcia steps over the arm.

6. Garcia pulls the arm up like a lever.

7. Garcia drops his body with the body mass directed down and backwards against Dolby.

ONE STEP PUNCHING TECHNIQUE III
1. Starting position.

2. Garcia delivers a punch: Dolby blocks with an inside double open hand block.

3. Dolby cocks his hand to deliver a knife hand strike.

4. Dolby executes the knife hand strike.

5. Dolby continues by executing a palm fist strike.

6. He finishes with an elbow strike.

ONE STEP PUNCHING TECHNIQUE IV

1. Starting position with Farber attacking.

2. Farber punches: Garcia moves to block.

3. Garcia executes an outside block and grabs the arm.

4. Garcia cocks the leg for a side kick.

5. Garcia executes a side kick.

ATTACKING TECHNIQUES I

1. Ready position. Farber will retreat and observe Garcia executing a series of attacking techniques.

2. Garcia leads with a reverse punch.

3. Garcia follows up with another reverse punch to the face.

4. Jamming — a front kick is executed.

5. Follow-up with a reverse punch.

6. Garcia grabs and cocks the leg for a heel kick to the head.

7. Garcia executes a heel kick to the head.

ATTACKING TECHNIQUES II

1. Ready position. Garcia retreats and Farber attacks.

2. Farber leads with a right reverse punch: Garcia blocks.

3. Garcia steps back again: Farber follows with an upper punch, faking a technique.

4. Farber follows up with a ridge hand to the head.

5. And finishes with a left hand reverse punch to the body.

NOTE: Attacking techniques are practiced slowly and with strong recall on the techniques. Both parties can learn greatly with the attack as well as the retreat.

CHAPTER

TWO

Stances

This chapter deals with the basic stances in Tang Soo Do. Stances are always taught in combination with footwork. In the initial phase of training, the beginning student is taught four fundamental stances.

The *Choon Bee Jaseh* is the first stance learned. For this stance, the student stands straight with feet together on one line about twelve inches apart. The feet are both facing forward as if on a pair of skis.

The second stance is the *Bal Moa Seo Kee Jaseh.* This is the position for attention. The student stands with both feet together with the heels and toes touching. This is the starting position for bowing and paying one's respects.

The third position is the *Chun Gul Jaseh* or forward stance. The forward stance is probably the single most important stance used in Tang Soo Do. It is from this stance that the student learns most of the basic defenses and how to move along the mat area, up and down and forwards and backwards. For the forward stance, the student stands with the left leg forward bent at the knee; the right leg is to the rear and remains straight. The feet are shoulder width apart with the rear foot as a slight forty-five degree angle. Facing forward, sixty percent of the body weight is on the front leg and forty percent of the weight is on the back leg. The shoulders, back and hips are straight, forward and level.

From this stance, the student learns how to move up and down the mat area. From this position, the student brings the rear foot forward with the knees bent, stepping out with the rear leg to the front and exchanging the same position with the rear foot now in the front. Sixty percent of the body weight always remains on the front, lead foot and forty percent always remains on the rear foot.

The fourth stance is the *Sa Ko Rip Jaseho* or horse stance. This stance looks like what it sounds. The feet are spread more than shoulder width apart with both legs bent at the knees and both feet in the same line, facing forward as if straddling a horse. This stance, for the most part, is the most strenuous stance utilizing the outside calf muscles and a majority of the hip muscles that are not normally used strenuously. The horse stance is used in forms more than in fighting.

Another stance that is not one of the basic four but a variation of the third stance or forward stance is the backward stance. The backward stance is derived from the forward stance with the exception that the rear leg is bent at the knee and at a forty five degree angle. In the forward stance, the rear leg is kept straight. The front leg position remains the same in both stances. The body weight is now distributed on both legs equally. The back stance is used primarily for blocking.

A variation of the back stance is the cat stance. In the cat stance, the back stance is assumed and the body weight is then shifted to sixty percent on the back foot and forty percent on the front. The heel of the front foot is raised and the front leg is then supported by the ball of the foot only. Note that the knee of the front leg is bent.

There are many stances in Tang Soo Do that are introduced to the student at an intermediate and advanced level. The *Bbachai Stance* and the *Kaihanzi*, for example, are beginning stances in two of the advanced forms of Tang Soo Do.

The free sparring stance is probably the most difficult stance for the student to acquire as it has no rigid form or guidelines. It cannot be derived from a text or through instruction but must come about as a product of actual free sparring. It is the stance which is most comfortable and allows for maximum freedom of action and movement. The angle of the posture and weight distribution of the feet will vary from individual to individual.

Chapter Four will illustrate how the various stances are applied in the movements utilized in the Hyungs (forms). In studying the Hyungs, close attention should be paid to the stances and their relationship to each other.

CHAPTER

THREE

Fundamental Blocking Techniques

There are five fundamental blocks in Tang Soo Do. Each of the five blocks will be discussed and demonstrated in this chapter. They are as follows: the inside block, the outside block, the high block, the low block and the straight forward block. The straight forward block often becomes a blocking strike which is known as the knife hand block which is one variation in Tang Soo Do.

In responding to an attack, using the two arms in the most natural way, all the basic blocks emanate from the natural flow of directions. Before undertaking the basic blocking movements, however, the student should understand the limitations of arm movements. All arm movements are encompassed within movements described by a complete arch of 360 degrees. To maximize the effectiveness of blocking and deflecting the attack; the student must develop a sense of the most appropriate circular or linear move in response to each attack. The most effective defense is usually the simplest and the most direct which is determined by the spontaineity, ease and speed with which it can be executed. Ed Parker, the noted pioneer of American Kenpo Karate, once remarked, "He who hesitates usually meditates in prone position." This advice, I feel, is most appropriate in regards to the principles of blocking. The beginning student should never feel that there is always a second chance but must train to execute his blocks effectively with naturalness and speed.

In the following photos, each of the five blocks are clearly illustrated. The student should practice each block repeatedly from every position and stance including sitting and prone positions. There are no limits to develop effective blocking techniques and this can be applied to every phase in studying the art of Tang Soo Do.

Also, I will cover briefly the basic chops and double blocks. Usually, they are utilized in Hyungs, (forms), but they are also effective tools in free sparring.

1. The inside block is the first block to be demonstrated:

1. The left hand is extended and the right hand is at the side of the head.

2. Front view.

3. The left hand draws to the left side and the right hand blocks the inside front of the body.

2. The outside block:

3. The high block:

4. The low block:

5. The straight forward block:

6. The double block:

Cocking

Block low.

Cocking.

Block high.

7. The chops:

CENTER CHOP

1. Beginning position for the center chop. The right hand is positioned across the body at a forty-five degree angle and held tight in preparation for impact. The left hand is extended behind the body also preparing for impact.

2. Final center chop position.

NOTE: Chops are used in and generally confined to Hyungs. They demonstrate style more than purpose. Under close observation, a knife hand block is one-half of a center chop.

3. Front view of the starting position.

4. Front view of the final position of the hands.

LOW CHOPS
1. Starting position.

2. Final position.

3. Front view of the starting position.

4. Front view of the final position.

NOTE: All chops are accomplished with a snapping motion. The hands are held firmly and resting in a ridged state.

CHAPTER

FOUR

Standing Kicks

FOOT STRIKES

Striking with the foot is the strongest tool the basic Tang Soo Do student possesses. All of Tang Soo Do revolves around the strike of the foot. As mentioned in the beginning of this text, sixty percent of Tang Soo Do is kicking so the natural consequence of this is foot striking. Foot striking is the root of Tang Soo Do. No matter how swift the kick or how much power is delivered behind its thrust, the foot strike is the end object of focus. The foot must be strong, rigid and properly placed to achieve this end result. One must continually practice basic foot positions.

1. "ROLL UPS" — Starting with feet flat on the floor, raise the heels up one inch, hold for two minutes and then raise them up two more inches and hold for two minutes. Then roll all the way up on the ball of the foot and hold for two minutes. Do not hold on to anything for balance, you must balance yourself. This exercise is used to build a strong foot.
2. "WALL FLEXES" — Beginning with a flat smooth wall. Place your toes on the wall and your feet on the floor. Keep working your feet until you are able to develop a ninety degree angle from the ball of the foot.
3. "BAG STRIKES" — One of the best methods to develop a strong foot (and hand) is to strike the heavy (100 lbs.) bag.

The best training is accomplished when the trainee has a pre-determined set of exercises to follow, such as fifteen front kicks (left and right leg) and twenty round kicks (spinning) left and right leg. Then execute slide-up round kicks (left and right). Take a two minute break. Beginning again with standing side kicks ten with the left and right leg. Then execute slide up side kicks — fifteen each leg and finally ten each leg with stepping back kicks. The above group of kicks is called a "training set". This set should be done before and after a normal work out. This is twice a day for each day you work out.

FOOT POSITIONS

1. Ball Foot
   a. Proper position.
   b. Proper placement of foot to target area.
   This is the correct position of the foot when it is properly executed. A good exercise to develop better foot posture as well as stronger feet is, while standing, raise yourself as high as possible on the balls of your feet. Relax, dropping down to your original standing position and raise yourself up again. This should be done in a series

of ten repetitions increasing the sets gradually as you become stronger. It is important to increase stress to produce more work but not strain against the muscles.

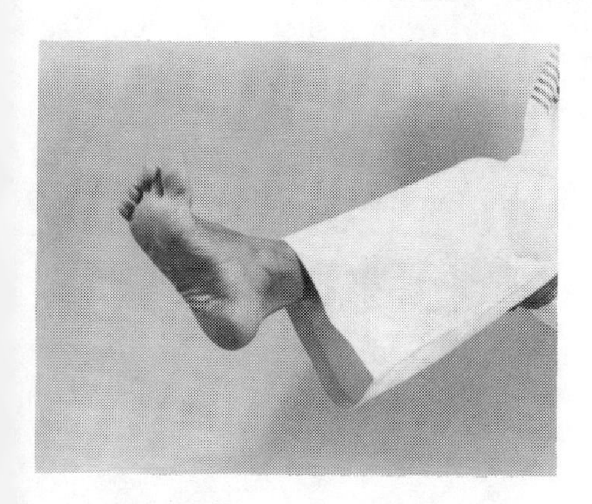

2. Palm Foot
   a. Proper position. Note that the striking area is the heel and ball of the foot combined.
   b. Proper striking techniques applied in the jumping crescent kick. When delivering an inside crescent kick or block, the striking surface is the instep portion of the foot. All such kicks in Tang Soo Do can be delivered from the ground as well as the jump kicks which will be covered later in this book. Kicks for the student can be practiced from a standing as well as sitting position.

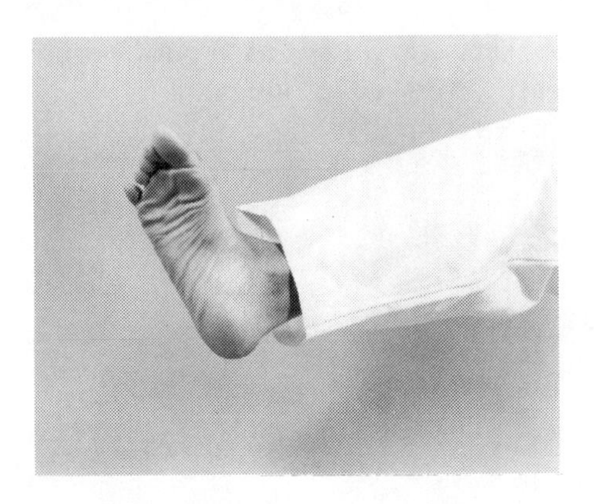

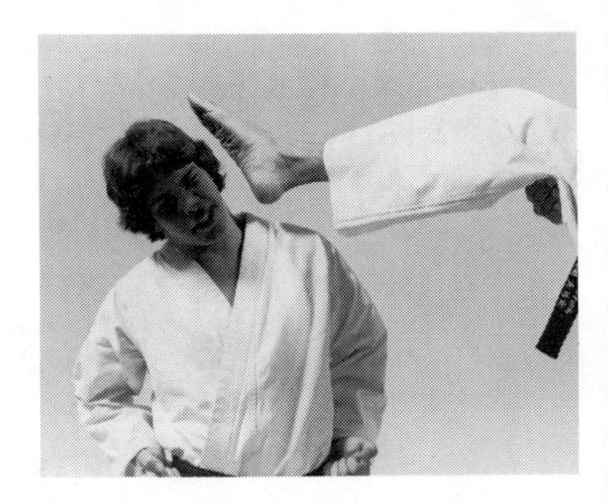

3. Knife Edge
   a. Proper striking position.
   b. Proper position for the flying side kick. This portion of the foot is used most frequently in kicking. By many, it is considered the strongest portion of the boot. It is used from a sitting and standing position and applied to the flying side kick, standing side kick, sitting side kick and outside crescent kick.

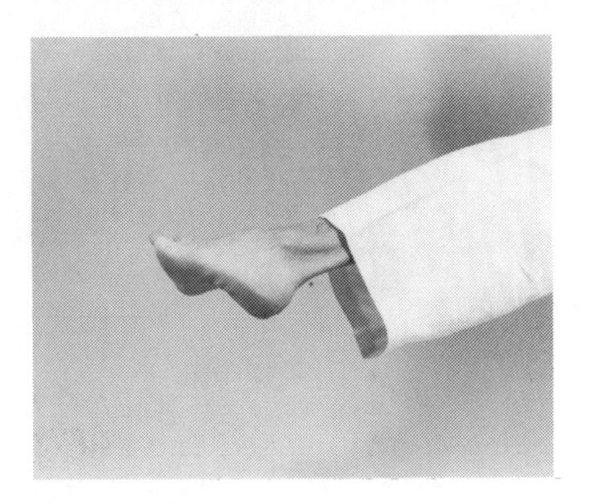

4. Heel
   a. Proper striking edge.
   b. The striking area is the flat back of the heel. The heel kick is a devastating kick when properly executed; however, correct leg position is of the utmost importance. The leg should be slightly bent and the foot rigid. This kick is applied in the spinning heel kick, standing heel kick, standing side kick and the back kick.
   c. A heel kick to the back of the head.

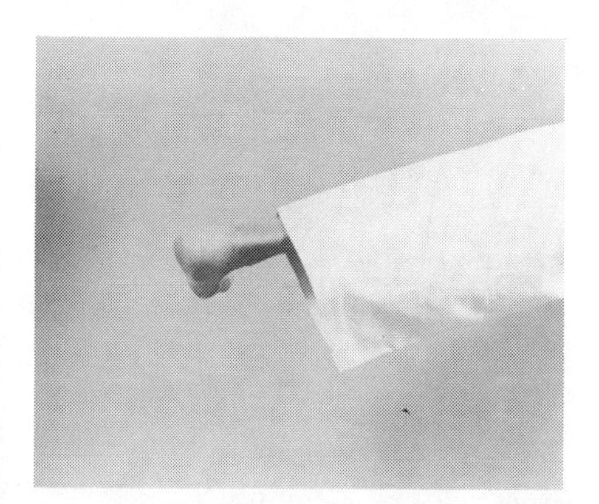

5. Instep
   a. The correct striking surface is the entire portion of the foot from the toes to the ankle. This strike is used in round kicks, roundhouse kicks and crescent kicks.
   b. A roundhouse kick to the temple.
   c. A round kick to the chest.
   In many instances, this kick is used in blocking.

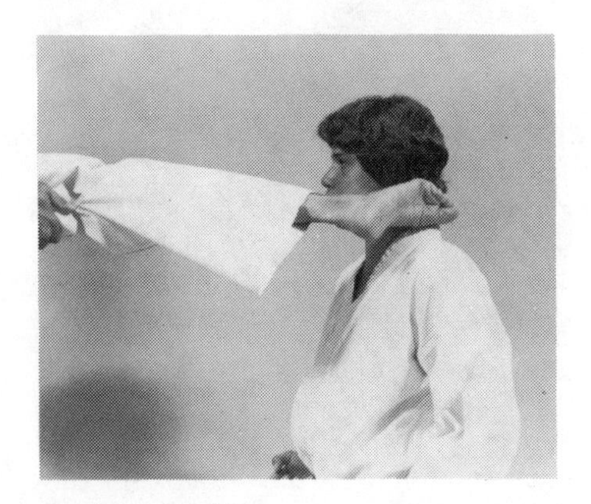

6. Knee
   a. Proper striking position.
      The knee is used when fighting in close proximity, because of this it is limited in usage although it is a very strong kick.
   b. A knee strike to the solar plexis. This is a devastating technique in Tang Soo Do.
   c. The knee kick is used to produce crunching results.

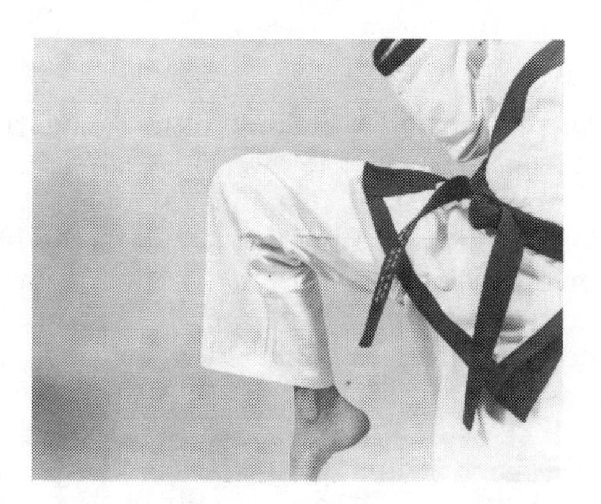

Standing Kicks

FRONT KICK

Tang Soo Do is principally a kicking style of fighting. Approximately sixty percent of all the strikes and blows in Tang Soo Do are derived from kicks. One's leg is approximately five times stronger than one's arm. The center of power for the kick in Tang Soo Do is in the hips. It is the thrust of the hips that give the kick its power. There are four basic kicks which will be discussed and illustrated. They are as follows: the front kick, the round kick, the side kick and the back kick. Each of these kicks, in turn, have three variations.

The first basic kick is the front kick. Starting off with the rear leg coming up, bring the knee to the chest in a cocked position, thrust the leg out directly in a pushing manner. Strike with the farthest extension of the ball of the foot. Recock the leg immediately after delivering the kick. It is important to note that recocking the leg is equally important as the kick itself. After recocking the leg, draw the leg back to the original position and resume a starting position again.

One variation of the front kick is the sliding up front kick. Start from a fighting position. The rear leg slides forward, the front leg comes up and the knee is cocked up to the chest. The leg is then thrust out for the kick. Recock the leg immediately and assume your original position.

A second variation of the front kick is the standing front kick.

Starting from a forward stance. Transfer about ninety percent of your body weight to the rear leg and cock the front leg up to the chest. Thrust the leg out for the kick, recock the leg, and resume your original position. In the standing front kick, there is no travelling but a shift in body weight.

A third variation of the front kick is the stepping front kick. In a stepping front kick, start off with the rear leg. After the leg is extended directly out in front of you and recocked, the leg is set down in front, constituting one full step in the kicking movement. This differs from the sliding up front kick which is completed in a half-step distance.

ROUND KICK

The second basic kick is the round kick or, more commonly known as, roundhouse kick. It is called a round kick because the body moves in a circular pattern. In contrast, the front kick and the back kick are based on linear movements. The spinning of the body and the roundhouse motion of the leg in this kick follows the same principle of dynamics as the roundhouse punch.

The three variations of the round kick are the standing round kick, the spinning round kick and the slide up round kick.

SIDE KICK

The spinning round kick is the third variation of the round kick. In the spinning round kick, start from a fighting stance. Turn the body and spin the rear leg 180 degrees around from behind to the target area or point of impact. No spinning round kick should be delivered in more than a 180 degree arch. In the spinning round kick, the rear leg must be cocked as the body pivots on the front leg. The leg is thrust out for the kick and recocked immediately. The leg can either be brought all the way back into the original position or set down in front directly after impact.

The third basic kick is the side kick. The side kick is designed to be delivered from the side. The student should practice this kick from any position moving forward or backwards. The primary portion of the foot used in the side kick is the outside heel. Start from a basic fighting stance. You may move into either a slide up side kick, a spinning side kick or a standing side kick. These are the three variations of the side kick.

The first variation, the slide up side kick, is considered to be the most devastating and powerful of all the basic kicks. A slide up side kick is most useful because the maximum amount of power is exerted from a minimum amount of effort. Starting from a fighting stance, slide the rear foot to the front, cock the foot leg up, deliver the leg straight, striking out with the heel of the foot. Recock the leg and resume your fighting stance. This kick is very useful in that the foot travels the shortest distance and the hips are in a strong position to receive the maximum amount of shock absorption. The powerful thigh and rear muscles, (the muscles developed by sprinters) are used to push away.

BACK KICK

The second variation is the spinning side kick. This kick begins with a pivot on the front foot. Bring the knee around in front of you, extend the leg out behind you and strike with the heel portion of the foot. Recock the leg immediately and set the leg either back into the original stance or drop it down in front of you.

The third variation is the standing side kick. This kick starts again from your fighting stance. The front leg is cocked with the knee off to one side of the body. Turn the body to a forty five degree angle. Aim with the hip and extend the leg back straight out, striking with the heel portion of the foot. Recock the foot and resume your fighting stance.

The fourth and last basic kick in Tang Soo Do is the back kick. This kick is limited in use because it is usually only delivered from a standing position.

SPINNING ROUND KICK
1. Starting position in a fighting stance.

2. Pivot around cocking the right leg upwards.

3. Extend the right out.

4. Recover your position with the right leg forward.

SLIDE-UP SIDE KICK
1. Starting position.

2. Rear leg slides up to the front.

3. Raise the right knee with the toes curled.

4. Extend the leg.

5. Recover.

6. Return the leg to the floor.

7. Step back with the rear leg.

SPINNING SIDE KICK

1. Starting position.

2. Pivot around bringing the knee up and keeping the toes curled.

3. Extend the leg driving it with the heel.

4. Recover your position with the right leg forward.

SLIDE-UP HEEL KICK
1. Starting position.

2. Cock the right leg up.

3. Swing the leg across and upwards striking the target.

4. Recover your position.

Jump Kicks

Jump kicks or flying kicks are the most devastating weapons within the Tang Soo Do practitioners' arsenal. Simply put, the kicking dynamics of body weight, velocity and snap are transferred to the air against the opponent. The end result is the most destructive Tang Soo Do strike.

All of the four basic kicks have a flying counterpart. In addition, there are also flying double kicks of a more advanced nature and more difficult to execute.

CHAPTER

FIVE

Hyungs [Forms]

Forms are the basic development of:

1. Balance

2. Power

3. Co-ordination

4. Endurance

5. Agility

BASIC FORMS I, II, & III were put together in their present form by Grand Master Hwang Kee in 1947. The reason for these forms (Hyungs) is to help the beginning student develop basic techniques. Before Basic Hyungs I, II, & III, most forms were too complicated for the beginning student.

Tang Soo Do forms are a logical progression from basic to more complicated techniques.

The *Pyong Ahn* forms, or the fourth forms, were constructed approximately around 1870. Within the *Pyong Ahn* forms, the beginning student is able to demonstrate that he has mastered balance and body control beyong the basic techniques. Additionally, the beginning student demonstrates concentration and meditation, freeing his mind from clutter and outside thoughts. The reason for the Hyungs, and the techniques they develop, is that they develop a non-verbal form of communication. They form a history of physical techniques, techniques put in patterns of communication, one blending into another, of kicks, punches and blocks. They develop reflexes and instinctive techniques which are essential later for free flowing unrestricted movement. They coordinate specific muscle groups that perform the best blocks or kicks and strikes. They develop over-all body endurance and timing, while they appear to the novice as some sort of restricted and stylized form, they really develop total freedom of body and mind.

> Into a soul absolutely free
> from thoughts and emotion,
> even the tiger finds no
> room to insert its fierce
> claws.
>
> *Ancient Saying*

Hyungs [Forms]

I. Basic Form One — introduces the beginning student to the low defense and stepping center punch. This form is basically simple in that the basic movement is a forward stance and movements of the feet are forward only. There are twenty-two stations in this form. The beginning student has to learn, low defense, forward stance and a center punch.

II. Basic Form Two — is much the same as Form One. Again forward stances, low defense is the basic ingredient; however, a high punch replaces all the center punches that Basic Form One possesses.

III. Basic Form Three — begins with a new defense; the outside block from a back stance is the primary defense used. Where the beginning student used center punches down the center of Form I and II, in form III, the side punch is used. Again the beginning student is adding one other basic strike to an ever building arsenal of defenses.

IV. Basic Form Four — begins a more complex set of movements. Within this form, a more offensive posture is taken. The first back knuckle strike is shown and chops are seen for the first time.

V. Basic Form Five — begins a new phase for the intermediate student. Duel strikes are seen for the first time as well as kicking and punching techniques.

VI. Within Form Six, the use of kick blocking is taught. Balance as well as duel striking is developed further.

VII. Much like Form Six, Form Seven develops much the same area.

VIII. For the intermediate student, Form Eight is the most complex. While this form is shorter, it is far more difficult. There are multiple changes of directions within this form.

BASIC FORM #1
GIECHO HYUNG IL BU
1. Ready Stance (Jun Bi)

2. Step out with left foot — Low Block Fold

3. 90° Turn — Low Block/Forward Stance

4. Stepping Center Punch/Forward Stance

5. Weight shift to left leg, right leg moves behind and across the body — Low Block Fold

6. 180° Turn — Low Block

7. Stepping Center Punch

8. Step out to left with left leg — Low Block Fold

9. 90° Turn — Low Block/Forward Stance

10. Stepping Center Punch/Forward Stance

11. Stepping Center Punch/Forward Stance

12. Stepping Center Punch/Forward Stance — *KIAI*

13. Left leg moves behind and across; head and shoulders turn to right — Low Block Fold

14. 270° Turn — Low Block/Forward Stance

15. Stepping Center Punch/Forward Stance

16. Weight shifts to left leg, right leg moves behind and across body — Low Block Fold

17. 180° Turn — Low Block/Forward Stance

18. Stepping Center Punch/Forward Stance

19. Step out with left leg — Low Block Fold

20. 90° Turn — Low Block/Forward Stance

21. Stepping Center Punch/Forward Stance

22. Stepping Center Punch/Forward Stance

23. Stepping Center Punch/Forward Stance — *KIAI*

24. Left leg moves behind and across body; head and shoulders turn — Low Block Fold

25. 270° Turn — Low Block/Forward Stance

26. Stepping Center Punch/Forward Stance

27. Right leg moves behind and across body — Low Block Fold

28. 180° Turn — Low Block/Forward Stance

29. Stepping Center Punch

30. Recover

31. Ready Stance (Jun Bi)

BASIC FORM #2
GIECHO HYUNG YI BU
1. Ready Stance (JUN BI)

2. 90° Turn — Low Block/Forward Stance

3. Stepping High Punch/Forward Stance

4. 180° Turn — Low Block/Forward Stance

5. Stepping High Punch/Forward Stance

6. 90° Turn — Low Block/Forward Stance

7. Stepping High Block/Forward Stance

8. Stepping High Block/Forward Stance

9. Stepping High Block/Forward Stance — *KIAI*

10. 270° Turn — Low Block/Forward Stance

11. Stepping High Punch/Forward Stance

12. 180° Turn — Low Block/Forward Stance

13. Stepping High Punch/Forward Stance

14. 90° Turn — Low Block/Forward Stance

15. Stepping High Block/Forward Stance

16. Stepping High Block/Forward Stance

17. Stepping High Block/Forward Stance — *KIAI*

18. 270° Turn — Low Block/Forward Stance

19. Stepping High Punch/Forward Stance

20. 180° Turn — Low Block/Forward Stance

21. Stepping High Punch/Forward Stance

22. JUN BI

FORM #3
GIECHO HYUNG SAHM BU
1. JUN BI

2. Outside Block Fold

3. 90° Turn — Outside Block/Back Stance

4. Stepping Center Punch/Forward Stance

5. Outside Block Fold during 180° Turn

6. Outside Block/Back Stance

7. Stepping Center Punch/Forward Stance

8. 90° Turn — Low Block/Forward Stance

9. Stepping Side Punch/Straddle Leg Stance

10. Spinning Bottom Fist/Straddle Leg Stance

11. Stepping Side Punch/Straddle Leg Stance — *KIAI*

12. Outside Block Fold during 270° Turn

13. Outside Block/Back Stance

14. Stepping Center Punch/Forward Stance

15. Outside Block Fold during 180° Turn

16. Outside Bock/Back Stance

17. Stepping Center Punch

18. 90° Turn — Low Block/Forward Stance

19. Stepping Side Punch/Straddle Leg Stance

20. Spinning Bottom Fist/Straddle Leg Stance

21. Stepping Side Punch/Straddle Leg Stance — *KIAI*

22. Outside Block Fold during 270° Turn

23. Outside block/Back Stance

24. Stepping Center Punch/Forward Stance

25. Outside Block Fold during 180° Turn

26. Outside Block/Back Stance

27. Stepping Center Punch/Forward Stance

28. JUN BI

Hyungs [Forms]

FORM #4
PYONG AN CHO DAN
1. JUN BI

2. 90° Turn — Low Block/Forward Stance

3. Stepping Center Punch/Forward Stance

4. 180° Turn — Low Block/Forward Stance

5. Grip Breaking Arm Twist/Back Stance

6. Right Foot Slides Back/Back Knuckle Fold

7. Back Knuckle

8. Stepping Center Punch/Forward Stance

9. 90° Turn — Low Block/Forward Stance

10. Knife-Hand Fold

11. Knife-Hand Block/Forward Stance

12. Stepping High Block/Forward Stance

13. Stepping High Block/Forward Stance

14. Stepping High Block/Forward Stance — *KIAI*

15. 270° Turn — Low Block/Forward Stance

16. Stepping Center Punch/Forward Stance

17. 180° Turn — Low Block/Forward Stance

18. Stepping Center Punch/Forward Stance

19. 90° Turn — Low Block/Forward Stance

20. Stepping Center Punch/Forward Stance

21. Stepping Center Punch&Forward Stance

22. Stepping Center Punch/Forward Stance — *KIAI*

23. Reinforced Low Chop Fold during 270° Turn

24. Reinforced Low Chop

25. Right foot moves forward 45° Turn — Reinforced Low Chop

26. Right foot moves behind and across body — 135° Turn — Reinforced Low Chop

27. Left foot moves forward 45° Turn — Reinforced Low Chop

28. JUN BI

FORM #5
PYONG AN YI DAN
1. JUN BI

2. Double Block Fold

3. Double Block/Back Stance

4. Mid-Point of Punch

5. Upward Punch

6. Left Foot Slides Back

7. Stepping with left foot — Side Punch

8. Double Block Fold

9. Double Block/Back Stance

10. Mid-Point of Punch

11. Upward Punch

12. Right Foot Slides Back

13. Stepping with right foot — Side Punch

14. Right foot stationary — Left foot moves forward — Hands right side in Double Block Fold

15. Hands switch to left side in Double Block Fold

16. Side Kick — Bottom Fist

17. Recover from #16 directly into Reinforced Center Chop

18. Stepping Reinforced Center Chop

19. Stepping Reinforced Center Chop

20. Midpoint Stepping Spear Hand

21. Spear Hand/Forward Stance — *KIAI*

22. Midpoint 270° Turn

23. Reinforced Center Chop

24. Right foot moves forward — 45° Turn — Reinforced Center Chop

25. Right foot moves behind and across body — 135° Turn/Reinforced Center Chop

26. Left foot moves forward — 45° Turn/Reinforced Center Chop

27. 45° Turn — outside Block/Forward Stance

28. Stepping Front Kick

29. Center Punch/Forward Stance

30. Outside Block/Forward Stance

31. Stepping Front Kick

32. Center Punch/Forward Stance

33. Mid-point of Stepping Reinforced Block

34. Reinforced Block/Forward Stance

35. Knife Hand Fold

36. Knife Hand Block/Forward Stance

37. 45° Turn — Stepping High Block

38. 135° Turn — Low Block/Forward Stance

39. Knife Hand Fold

40. Knife Hand Block/Forward Stance

41. 45° Turn — Stepping High Block — *KIAI*

42. JUN BI

FORM #6
PYONG AN SAHM DAN
1. JUN BI

2. Outside Block/Back Stance

3. Right foot Slides forward — Right hand moves forward to position in front of groin

4. Mid-point Double Block

5. Double Block

6. Mid-point Double Block

7. Double Block

8. Outside Block/Fold during 180° Turn

9. Outside Block/Back Stance

10. Left foot slides forward — Left hand moves forward to position in front of groin

11. Mid-point Double Block

12. Double Block

13. Mid-point Double Block

14. Double Block

15. Reinforced Block Fold (Knuckle to Knuckle) during 90° Turn

16. Reinforced Block/Forward Stance

17. Mid-point of stepping Hand Spear

18. Hand Spear/Forward Stance

19. Left foot moves forward as 360° Turn begins

20. Left foot continues moving forward during 360° Turn

21. Bottom Fist/Straddle Leg Stance

22. Mid-point stepping Center Punch

23. Center Punch/Forward Stance — *KIAI*

24. 180° Turn

25. Fists lower to hips and foot touches mat simultaneously

26. Pause

27. High Inside Crescent Kick with right leg

28. Right leg cocked after Crescent Kick

29. Right foot stamp — upper body turns and block with upper arm and shoulder

30. Back Knuckle/Straddle Leg Stance

31. Right fist returns to hip/Straddle Leg Stance moving about 45° to our left. We'll view the next ten moves from a slight angle.

32. High Crescent Kick with Left Leg

33. Left leg cocked after Crescent Kick

34. Left leg stamp — upper body turns blocking with upper arm and shoulder

35. Back Knuckle/Straddle Leg Stance

36. Left fist returns to hip/Straddle Leg Stance

37. High Crescent Kick with right leg

38. Right leg cocked after Crescent Kick

39. Right foot stomp — upper body turns to right blocking with upper arm and shoulder

40. Back Knuckle/Straddle Leg Stance

41. Fist turns over during mid-point of stepping center punch

42. Center Punch/Forward Stance

43. Right foot moves forward and out to Straddle Leg Stance

44. Mid-point of 180° Turn

45. Right Hand Punch over left shoulder — Straddle Leg Stance

46. Mid-point of leap to the right

47. Left hand Punch over right shoulder as you land/Straddle Leg Stance — *KIAI*

48. JUN BI

FORM #7
PYONG AN SA DAN
1. JUN BI

2. Double Block Fold
Midpoint Double Knife Hand Block

3. Double Knife Hand Block/Back Stance

4. Turning in Back Stance — Double Block Fold

5. Double Knife Hand Block/Back Stance

6. 90° Turn — Stepping with left foot — fists crossing at chest

7. Crossed Arm Low Block/Forward Stance

8. Right foot moving forward — Reinforced Block Fold (Knuckle to Knuckle)

9. Reinforced Block/Forward Stance

10. Left foot moving forward — both hands to right side of body

11. Side Kick — Bottom Fist Recocking Side Kick

12. Forearm Attack/Forward Stance

13. Quick Shift into Back Stance — 180° Turn

14. Left Leg Slides Up

15. Side Kick — Bottom Fist

16. Recocking Side Kick

17. Forearm Attack/Forward Stance

18. Simultaneous High and Low Knife Hand Blocks — Forward Stance — Right Leg Forward

19. Pivot into Forward Stance — Left leg forward as left hand raises to High Knife Hand Block and right hand chops parallel to mat

20. Stepping Front Kick

21. Recocking Front Kick — Folding for lunging Back Knuckle

22. Landing after lunging Back Knuckle

23. After Stepping to Left Rear — ingo Forward Stance — Hands cross and reach under "collar"

24. Fists tighten on "collar"

25. Fists turn over and pull apart
Stepping Front Kick

26. Right High Punch/Back Stance

27. Reverse Center Punch/Forward Stance

28. Turning 90° with right foot — Hands cross and reach under "collar"/ Forward Stance

29. Fists tighten on "collar"
Fists turn over and pull apart

30. Stepping Front Kick

31. Left High Punch/Back Stance

32. Reverse Center Punch/Forward Stance

33. 45° Turn — Reinforced Block Fold

34. Reinforced Block/Back Stance
Note Cat Stance
Back Straight

35. Stepping Forward with Right Foot —
Reinforced Block Fold
Reinforced Block/Back Stance

36. Stepping Forward with Left Foot —
Folding for Reinforced Block
Reinforced Block/Back Stance

37. Left Hand Grabs Throat/Back Stance

38. Both Hands Grab Throat/Forward Stance

39. Both hands frop to meet right knee as it comes sharply upward — *KIAI* Note left leg slightly bent

40. Note hands snap across knee Note balance

41. Turning and Folding for Reinforced Center Chop
Reinforced Center Chop

42. 90° Turn Midpoint
Reinforced Center Chop

43. JUN BI

FORM #8
PYONG AN OH DAN
1. JUN BI

2. Outside Block Fold

3. 90° Turn stepping out with left leg — Outside Block/Back Stance

4. Punch Across Body/Back Stance

5. Right leg slides up — Hands come to right side

6. Fold for Outside Block

7. 90° Turn — Stepping out with right leg Outside Block/Back Stance

8. Punch Across Body/Back Stance

9. Left foot slides up — Hands come to left side

10. Step forward with right leg — Reinforced Block/Forward Stance

11. Stepping forward with left leg — fists cross at chest

12. Cross-arm Block/Forward Stance

13. Weight shifts to back stance — fists, still crossed, are drawn back

14. Shifting weight to forward stance, high crossed arm block, hands open

15. Rotate hands so that left hand is on top of the right hand — elbows bend and pull in toward body

16. Finger jab at mid-point of stepping center

17. Center Punch/Forward Stance — *KIAI*

18. 180° Turn

19. High Crescent Kick

20. Crescent Kick Recocked — Folded for Low Block
Low Block/Straddle Leg Stance

21. Head Turns 180° – Arms fold/Straddle Leg Stance

22. Back Hand with left hand/Straddle Leg Stance

23. Stepping through with right leg High Crescent Kick making contact with left hand

24. Forearm attack/Straddle Leg Stance

25. Left leg moves behind right leg — shifting weight into the Reinforced Back Knuckle

26. Step out with left leg into Back Stance, Fist lowers and turns 90°

27. Fist is turned back sharply as it makes a short but very snappy punch upward

28. Right leg steps through — pushing off with left leg, leap high in the air, crossing arms and legs

29. Arms and legs are crossed as you land

30. 90°Turn — step out with right leg, folding for Reinforced Block
Prepare for change in direction

31. Left leg moves across — arms folded for block
Low Knife edge Block/Back Stance

32. Weight shifts to Forward Stance — Right arm extended forward — hand open and palm up

33. Right hand closes and turns, palm down. Left hand in Knife edge position on right shoulder

34. Right fist pulls back briskly, as left hand Knife edge travels down right arm in a scissors type action

35. Left foot slides in — Right fist turns 90° as it lowers

36. Right fist turns back, punching sharply upward

37. Arms fold

38. With arms still folded, pivot on balls of both feet 180°
Double Back Knuckle

39. Right leg raises as right fist blocks down

40. Stepping out with right leg in Forward Stance — Left arm extended — Hand open and palm up

41. Left hand closes and turns palm down — draws back sharply while right hand Knife edge travels down the left arm and right fist closes just prior when right arm is straightened. Weight shifts to a Back Stance

42. Recover

43. JUN BI

CHAPTER

SIX

Training Techniques

I. Exercise

II. Weights

III. Water — kicks, punches

IV. Daily Dozen

1.	Front Kick	12
2.	Round Kick	12
3.	Side Kick	12
4.	Back Kick	12
5.	Spinning Back	12
6.	Stepping Back Kick	12

Totaling 72 kicks daily.
144 kicks on the right and left side.

V. Running — Monday, Wednesday & Friday — Sprint Tuesday and Thursday — 2 miles.

TRAINING

The foundation to training begins with simple exercise. In Tang Soo Do, there are various stages of exercise. The student that begins his Tang Soo Do training, is introduced initially to stretching exercises. The first simple exercise is standing straight up, feet together, bending at the waist and touching the fingertips to the floor in a bouncing repetition manner. Keeping the knees straight, the back straight and bending only at the hips, bounce approximately ten times until fingers can touch the floor. After this is completed, the body is straightened up again, hands placed on the hips, and the hips are rotated in a circular motion. This is to increase flexibility and agility within the hip muscles. Remember, Tang Soo Do emanates most of the power from the hips.

The second exercise is from the same position standing up, feet together crossing the left foot over the top of the right or the right foot over the top of the left. Bending over again at the hips, keeping the back straight and touch the fingers to the floor. As you will be able to tell from utilizing this exercise, one leg is going to be stretched more than the other. This exercise is also done approximately ten times with the back straightened, body erect, rotating at the hips. Then switch the leg back over again with the opposite side over. This is the basic exercise that is introduced to the beginning student.

The next exercise is sitting on the floor, legs straight out in front with the feet together from the toes all the way back, bending over at the hips, keeping the back straight, trying to achieve touching the chin to the knee cap, with the arms extended out and wrapped around the ankles. This again increases flexibility in the back of the legs and the lower back. From this position, the student then separates the legs approximately on a forty-five degree angle and from here touches the chin and tried to tough the center of the floor in front. This exercise again is for the hip joint, lower back and the muscles of the leg. These are the basic stretching exercises for a student who is within his first month of training. From there, other various exercises such as standing straight up with the back against the wall and utilizing a partner. Extend your leg out in front of you and have your partner lift the leg all the way up past the head to touch the foot to the wall behind you. It is best illustrated by saying that you are standing still on one foot and the other foot is up in the air touching the wall above you. This is going to achieve the maximum amount of stretching and flexibility so that you are able to kick at any height or level. From this position with your back flat against the wall, you turn to the side position with one foot on the round and the other foot out to your side. Your partner is going to lift that foot up to where it is parallel to the floor at first, level with the head second, and above the head afterwards. From this position, to achieve more flexibility the hip, the leg is walked around to the wall in front of you. This achieves a round kick position. Walking back out to the side is the side kick position and walking behind you and touching the wall is the back kick position. This exercise is done with both legs. This is a bit more advanced than the initial sitting on the floor technique. Also, to achieve more flexibility within the inner portion of your legs, a very good exercise is to sit on the floor, bringing the soles of your feet together in front of you, directly in front of the groin area with your knees elevated off the ground. Have your partner slowly put his hands on your knees and press them apart to where you achieve absolute flexibility in the groin area. This is an exercise that requires a lot of time and a lot of training. However, it can be achieved if the basic student practices this continually. Another good leg exercise for training in Tang Soo Do is starting from a fighting stance, left leg forward, right leg straight out behind you, swinging the right leg, keeping it straight above the head for anywhere from ten to fifteen repetitions. You swing the leg and keep it straight almost kicking directly over your head. This builds up the muscles in the stomach, in the back, in the hip as well as stretching them at the same time. This can be reversed so the opposite leg is done fifteen times.

WEIGHTS

Weights are most beneficial to the Tang Soo Do practitioner if they are utilized for the legs, keeping in mind that the legs are five times stronger than the arms. The legs also have to be five times stronger for delivery and recock than the arms, because you don't have the dexterity in the legs that you have in the arms. I won't dwell much on weights. However, some of the basic weight exercises that can be utilized are to use a one or two pound weight, whichever constitutes more of a challenge wrapped around the ankle. Using a hand rail or door knob or something to hold onto, execute leg raises. Leg raises start directly out in front of you, with fifteen repetions of elevating your leg directly in front, back to the floor and rest. Fifteen repetitions in this way, is going to enhance the quickness of your front kick and just simply the quickness in the important cocking movement. From the same position, the leg raises in sets of fifteen out to the right side, directly out to your side, parallel to the hip. Fifteen repetitions of this will enhance the cocking position of your side kick. And likewise execute the same exercise, from a standing straight up position, raising your leg up behind you. This will cause the body to lean a little bit, raise your leg up behind you as high as you can, lowering it down slowly. All these exercises are to be done very slowly until you can feel a little strain in the leg. This is not to say that you push your leg to where you strain it, but you must feel the strain. Remember, no gain without pain.

As far as punching power is concerned, it is better to stay away from weight to utilize strength in your punches. The very best way to build your punches is by just punching using bags, gravel, sand, or some object that will be able to absorb your shock. That will conclude my comments on weight.

WATER EXERCISES

Water exercises are very beneficial for developing punches and kicks. Finding a swimming pool and placing yourself in the water to where the water is level with the neck, begin with your front kicks. In a fighting stance, the water is going to serve as the very best resistance and also teach you the shortest distance between two points in the delivery of your kicks. Execute thirty-five repetitions of front kicks in the water.

Anywhere from seventy-five to one hundred for the advanced student executing both kicks. Maintain your balance and deliver your kick as fast and as hard as you can in the water. This holds true for the punching techniques. From a fighting stance in the water, you can practice your reverse punch, throwing it one hundred to two hundred times in the water, left and right. Your back fist one hundred to two hundred times in the water, left and right side. Your ridgehand one hundred to two hundred techniques, left and right hand side. With the ridgehand technique, not only should you throw it parallel in the water, but throw it straight up from under as a swinging underneath ridgehand, or a reverse chop.

Chops are the same thing, throwing backhand chops and overhand chops. Executing them one hundred to two hundred times in the water is not anywhere near too much.

THE DAILY DOZEN

Everyday, whether you are at the karate studio or not, all students should execute the daily dozen. This is how the daily dozen goes: Starting from a front kick position, in a fighting stance, execute twelve front kicks (right leg) twelve front kicks (left leg) with a one minute breather. Round kicks — twelve round kicks, spinning round kicks from the right leg and twelve round kicks, spinning round kicks from the right leg and twelve round kicks from the left leg with a one minute breather. Side kicks — starting off (this is a slide up side kick) with the right leg, twelve slide up side kicks, switching — twelve slide up side kicks with the left leg with a two minute breather. Going into the back kicks, standing back kicks, twelve right leg, twelve left leg, with a two minute breather. Spinning back kick, twelve with the right leg, twelve with the left leg. Take a three minute breather. The last kick will be the stepping back kick — twelve with the right leg, twelve with the left leg. If you will note you have executed seventy-two kicks per leg, that is 144 kicks. I think that the daily dozen is a most beneficial in that just being able to get through all 144 kicks is a challenge. But as you will be able to tell after one or two months, each one of these kicks for the duration of the entire exercise (all 144 kicks) will make you feel stronger and faster. The daily dozen is done without a partner, without anyone's assistance; the only thing you need is a stop watch for the rest intervals.

After approximately six months of building and developing the daily dozen, it is very beneficial for an intermediate student to start executing all these kicks against a heavy bag, so you start learning resistance, feeling what it is like to kick an object and getting a response from it. However, after you have executed all 144 kicks without a bag or a target, you will learn, as time goes on, when you start hitting the bag or hitting a target, it's like starting all over again. For as much thrust, there has to be an equal recock action after the initial shock.

RUNNING

The best schedule I can suggest for running, while training in Tang Soo Do, would be breaking the week down into a five day week, giving yourself two days rest on the weekends. Mondays, Wednesdays and Fridays, you practice sprinting. Sprint 100 yards. Initially do not sprint for time, but as time goes on, attempt to sprint the 100 yards to achieve a shorter time lapse. This is to be done Monday, Wednesday, and Fridays. If you are going to sprint this 100 yards, do it no more than four times each day (four times on Monday, four times on Wednesday, four times on Friday. Between each 100 yard sprint, give yourself a ten minute rest to stretch, walk it out and work on your flexibility. On Tuesdays and Thursdays, your primarily concerned with endurance, my suggestion here is a two mile run, with some hills up, some hills down, and a lot of straight away. Your only concern within the two mile run is running for time.

If you find yourself running this two miles in more than fifteen minutes, you are running entirely too slow. You must increase the speed and keep in mind the fact that at the end of all runs, you need to devote at least fifteen minutes to flexibility exercises. Those are the exercises we started off with which is basically stretching. All running should be finished off with stretching exercises.

CHAPTER

SEVEN

Sparring Techniques

From the emptiness we come, to the emptiness we go. Our life is but a spark in the night and our death but the setting of the sun. Since both heaven and earth's beginning, this has always been the way. What then is the cause for fear?

FREE SPARRING

PHASE I

This chapter begins with going back to the basics. In the beginning of the book, six attitudes were discussed and developed. Consciousness was the first. When fighting or sparring, one must be conscious of what is to be achieved. Is a simple technique your goal or is a definitive strike your end? One must be very conscious of what one is doing in training at all times. Working out for the sake of working out is not enough to reach a goal. Goals are the second step within the attitudes as stated from the beginning of this book. In free sparring, your goal is quicker reflexes, more endurance and control of your adversary. The self-sacrifice comes into focus while training, how much time you are willing to pay for a stronger quicker body. There is go gain without some pain, working out is painful because muscles grow tired and the mind begins to wander off into easier ways.

In free sparring, self-indulgence and achievement comes to the trainee as one. Before you are able to self-indulge, you must have achieved something, it may be a faster round kick or a complex hand technique.

The duty of all your expertise is to constantly refine your technique. Keep trying new forms of travel for your attack, and, of course, your main duty is always be aware of self-defense, that is why you started Tang Soo Do.

PHASE II

Meditation is a necessary must for a fighter, simply because mental focus is what separates humans from machines. It is very healthy for a fighter to spend hours of training alone without the presence of others. Practicing attacking techniques across a mat (within the training school) alone for hours is most beneficial. The reward will be that your attack is foreign to your opponent and you, as a fighter, will have inner confidence because of repetition.

A level of sub-conscious mental stamina will develop also from meditation. Mental stamina takes the form of having new vigor with your attack. When you draw an attack on your adversary, and, for some reason, it is deflected, you begin a new attack with the same vigor. Your opponent begins to think, "this guy never gets tired and never stops his aggression."

That is the reward of mental stamina. The reason that this should be sub-conscious is that a reflex is a better action than a slowly thoughtout plan of reaction.

PHASE III

Phase three begins a strong confidence stage of development. Now begins the physical work. The Tang Soo Do fighter needs speed, power, combination and strategy. Some of the following photos demonstrate training aids for the fighter.

To develop speed, a cross section of wind sprints and lunges should be practiced for that initiated (first) move. From a fighting position, push from the rear leg and raising the front leg 1/4 of an inch off the ground, lunge. Lunges should be done hours on end. This is very boring, but the end result is a faster first move on your opponent.

To develop power, again, we go back to the heavy bag; here as stated before, many combinations must be employed to obtain power.

PHASE IV

In sparring, begin with the learning of one step punching techniques. One step punching techniques are the beginning of the Tang Soo Do's basic introduction to free sparring for the student. He now has a partner, he is responsible for what that partner does to him as well as for what he does to that partner. In one step fighting, all movements toward your partner are made at the command of your partner. For instance, your partner steps back into a fighting stance, cocking his right hand, ready to punch you in the face. He will only move forward and punch you when you execute the proper command letting him know, I am ready for you to step forward and punch now, so that you are able to fix in your mind exactly what technique, exactly what block, exactly what defense, you're going to execute against this attack. This is very primitive and this is very elementary, but this is the beginning to free sparring. After two beginning students have accomplished the basic elements of one step punching, the next phase in their training is called attacking techniques apart.

In this phase, we take the two beginning students, put one on one side of the mat and the other on the other side of the mat inside the karate studio approximately twenty feet apart. They are both instructed to get into a fighting stance, from here on but the instructors command, one student is told to execute five to ten attacking kicks and punches across the mat toward his partner. His ultimate goal is to execute at least five or six front kicks, round kicks, side kicks, back kicks as he is moving across the mat, getting closer and closer to his partner. His partner's training benefit at this point is that he is able to see an adversary, an attacker,

coming toward him throwing various types of techniques. As his partner gets close, he gets ready, the closer he gets to throwing the punches and kicks he is able to see what block or deflection he should utilize. This is attacking techniques apart. From here, the two basic students are put together close as they were in one step punching, with the exception they are going to do attacking techniques together, alternating, and taking turns. First, one basic student moves across the mat executing his kicks and his punches toward his partner as his partner backs up, not trying to overrun his partner, not trying to actually strike his partner, utilizing his partner only as a moving target, executing attacking techniques as he is going and his partner is backing up, slowly blocking, deflecting, learning foot work, learning how to retreat, learning how to side step. When they get to one side of the mat the same operation is reversed, except it is the other student's turn to throw the techniques and the attacking student's turn to withdraw, blocking, deflecting the techniques coming at him.

The advantage to this training method is that both students are afforded an opportunity to see an attack coming at them and slowly they are able to make mistakes and learn from their own mistakes. When your partner throws a front kick and you block with a high block, you are going to get kicked in the stomach.

From this phase, they're able to increase their speed, increase their power, increase their blocking and striking techniques. After approximately one month of this type of attacking technique back and forth across the mat, the students are encouraged by their instructor not only to travel in a direct line backward and forward but to incorporate side stepping and moving into circular movements. This is the beginning of free sparring. They are able to move laterally as well as circularly. After approximately two months of attacking techniques back and forth, the instructor will teach his basic student sparring techniques from an attacking position backward and forward utilizing only hand techniques. The purpose for this is, the basic student, like a child, is not able to coordinate his hands and feet at first. So, we have to develop one or the other. It doesn't matter if you start with the kicks or the hands. It is this instructor's preference to start teaching the hand techniques first. Two students are paired up together with attacking techniques back and forth across the mat using hands only. From there you are going to learn that if you and your partner are approximately four or five feet apart, for you to be able to reach out and touch him or strike him with either hand, you are going to have to: deceive him on your initial move and: have deceptive hands coming towards him. You have to fake with one hand for instance, throwing a left hand punch, having him block high, when you strike toward his face and follow up with a reverse punch underneath. Also, you must be able to realize, as you are doing these techniques, that your feet must move when your hands move. You can't throw the hand techniques being five feet apart and be a threat to your partner. Those hands have to move in the precise moment when your partner's defenses are relaxed or moving into another phase. From the hand techniques, practicing back and forth across the mat, the next phase would be kicking techniques only. This instructor likes to have his students put their hands behind your back, wrap their hands around their belt with their chest, face and body completely exposed. Now, free sparring utilizing kicks only with your hands behind your back is going to teach you two things. It is going to teach you how to use your body to block, you can use your shoulders, you can use your back and you can use your legs, but one thing is for certain, when you are blocking with your body, that means you have to absorb shock. If your partner is executing a kick and if you are not utilizing your hands to block, the very best move for you is to move away. With the hands tied behind your back, the student is able to learn to throw his kicks only when he anticipates being able to strike his target. Consequently, utilizing the legs to block is going to cause certain pain to the insteps unless you're using the feet to block. After sparring, utilizing the hands only for awhile and then utilizing the feet only for awhile, the basic student, in a very controlled environment, is taught sparring with protective gear, head protection and hand protection under close supervision of the chief instructor. Many months pass before free sparring is allowed with open hands and open feet.

My philosophy about fighting can be readily examined if you understand my interpretation of what fighting means. There are two types of fighting. One is sport fighting. Sport fighting involves a mentality that leads one to fight for money, trophies and fame. I admire this form of fighting because this person is a professional and can apply his trade as needed. However, in every aspect of a great sport fighter there is also a little of the survival fighter. Survival fighting involves the ability to devastate when necessary.

I consider these the four basic ingredients in fighting:

1. Stance — solid footing and footwork.
2. Aggressiveness — expression of physical presence.
3. Technique — effective technique.
4. Relaxation — mental state of mind

After the above have been controlled, fighting only has to be practiced.

My development in fighting started with one of the world's best fighters, Chuck Norris. Norris appealed to me as a model fighter because he kept to simple and effective techniques. There was no fancy stuff, just basic kicking and punching techniques with follow-up combinations, refined and elevated to a very high level.

Sparring Techniques

SPARRING

My second level of training in sparring or free fighting was taught by Mike Stone. Mike Stone emphasized basically three areas in training champions. One was endurance, the second combinations and techniques and the third an exchange of ideas with other style and martial artist.

Endurance — Endurance means staying in shape. The best way to get in shape for fighting is to have sessions of free sparring, for instance, beginning with a two-minute round, five rounds your first week. The second week progressing to three-minute rounds, for five rounds, until you are eventually able to work your way up to fifteen three-minute rounds of continuous sparring with various sparring partners. It is very important that while training and sparring, you have different partners to spar with, not the same person who constantly learns your habits and your faults or you learning their habits and their faults. There has to be an exchange and variety.

Combinations — combinations are combinations in fighting; for instance, a few basic combinations begin with a fighting stance, leading off with a left hand jab, followed up by a right hand reverse punch, to be followed up by a front kick, to be followed up by a round kick, to be followed up by a basic spinning back kick, coming out of the back kick with a back knuckle reverse punch. That is a one combination basic technique.

Another basic combination technique to practice would be to start from a fighting stance again, extending out the front leg into a front kick, or a standing front kick recock, set it down, followed by another front kick, recock, set it down, jabbing with the right hand, reverse punch with the left hand, grabbing with both hands pulling as if you are pulling your opponent down to a knee thrust to the face. Another combination technique would be starting from a fighting stance, faking a right hand forward, jabbing, recocking, spinning immediately into a heel kick, coming out of the heel kick with a spinning round kick, spinning heel kick, spinning round kick, with all three techniques at a very high level to be followed up by the last spinning round kick, reverse punch, and a back knuckle punch. These are just some of the basic combinations that can be practiced. Some of the other combinations that can be practiced, would take us back to our stances, such as a fighting stance. One of the very best practicing combinations to practice is shuffling forward, bringing the rear foot to the front, stepping out with the front foot, rear foot to the front, and stepping out with the front foot. This is almost a half step movement; half a step forward, half a step out. After the basic movement is learned where the shoulders don't rise, the hips and head stay on the same level, and the body does not change or alter direction. This movement should progress into a fast shuffle. From here, every one of the basic combinations should begin. One of the more complex combinations would be something on the order of starting off with a quick immediate shuffle forward, cocking the right leg up for a side kick extending the side kick out, immediately after the side kick is out, recocking it, following up with a back knuckle with the lead hand, from here, *immediately* following up with a front kick, from here immediately following up with a lunging front kick and possibly a flying side kick. This type of a complex combination should be employed after the basic stepping through techniques are perfected. It was stated earlier that the four basic ingredients for fighting are: stance, aggressiveness, technique and relaxation. Taking one by one, beginning with stances, we can see that a fighting stance has to be perfected where the fighter is able to sprint like a track runner. He has to sprint forward, backwards, and sideways. Stances should be practiced in front of a mirror in all four directions. Maybe a week practicing only side stepping to the right. Otherwise, looking at yourself directly in the mirror, seeing your stance, observing your profile, observing your hand positioning, you're going to only parry to the right in case the attack comes forward. You have to side step to the right, this means that you must start stepping with possibly the front leg first. To maintain balance, step off with the front leg and drag the rear leg across. That's practicing to the right. Also, from a stance, you should be able to parry, using the left hand or using the right hand without moving the feet whatsoever. All parries are employed as a very, very, very last resource. After the basic stance is accomplished where there is comfort and speed, mobility and agility aggressiveness is the next phase. Aggressiveness in your fighting is that ability to turn on full speed, turn on half speed, turn on slow speed when you need to, as well as giving an expression of command presence over your opponent. Command presence is simply that presence which indicates that you are in charge of the fight. You are the one that is going to direct the path of this fight, You are going to direct the violence. You are going to direct the passiveness in the fight. Your physical presence alone is not enough; your state of mind in aggressiveness has to be like a light switch that you need to turn on, or turn off. I need to turn it on a little bit, I need to turn it off a little bit. With aggressiveness, the only training in Tang Soo Do, I have found, has been strictly meditation and self control. Those two techniques, once they are developed, emanates into aggressiveness.

The third phase of the four basic ingredients is technique. Once again, we are back to our combinations and effective techniques. The very best way to find out if a technique does or does not work is to try it. If you tried a technique five times, or ten times and it has a high percentage of working or a high percentage of deception to your opponent, it is probably valid. Keeping in mind that all of the techniques can be valid simply if they are perfected properly. The last phase is relaxation. Relaxation is comfort in the deployment of all the prior phases, comfort in your stance, comfort in your aggressiveness, and comfort in your technique. This is a mental state; relaxing is not a physical relaxation. It is a mental relaxation; the body can only be fluent. The body can only anticipate when it is relaxed. It can't operate under stress, it can't operate under a second guess. In Tang Soo Do, in the beginning of all training at the studio, students are seated and told, for anywhere from ninety seconds to two minutes, to keep their eyes closed, back straight, and sit in an erect position. One must relax, getting the body and mind in tune with one another, getting the body and mind in harmony with one another, and also getting the body and mind in harmony with the surroundings. Once relaxation is accomplished, all of the techniques, all of the physical training, all of the combinations, funnel into a head. Now you can see perfection in the practice of the art, perfection in the teaching of the art and perfection in the exchange of the art.

Before closing this chapter on sparring, I'd like to take this opportunity to offer suggestions to the free fighter or to the free sparring person whose opponent is either an aggressor on the street of whom you know or a fellow student. When practicing your fighting, you are in your stance, you are comfortable, you are relaxed, and you have the proper amount of aggressiveness. The single thing you have to watch most in your opponent is the center mass of his body. If you are standing beyond one arm's length, as you should be from your opponent, nothing can touch you. No portion of his body, no extremity of his body can touch you without moving the center mass. The center mass is that portion of the body below the neck down to the groin area. One of the absolutely biggest faults that the basic student, has when he watches an opponent, is he watches the eyes or he watches the hands. Eyes have not hurt anyone in history. Hands can hurt, but hands can only reach you after the center mass moves forward. So from your fighting stance, it is not necessary to look into the face, it is necessary to look at the center portion of the chest, if that moves forward, you move back. If that moves back, you move forward. If that moves sideways, you move into a circular position. This is best achieved by one simple technique in practice. A classical Tang Soo Do method would be to have two students assume a fighting stance, using a belt, (preferably a white belt) to tie the two students approximately four feet apart. From here, all of their techniques have to be practiced in a fight situation. As you will be able to tell with the belt tied between you, you cannot move away from one another, you can only move toward one another, the belt should be that distance to allow over extension or a reach on either student's behalf and to be able to touch the other student. After the belt is tied onto the two students, circular movement is taught here, extension is taught here, and most important, watching the center mass is taught here. If by tugging the belt one way or the other, you are able to tell that the opponent cannot touch you without moving his center mass. Another suggestion would be, while fighting, avoid making eye contact with your opponent, watch everything about him, except his eyes. Some people are able to intimidate, and read expressions in your face, by just watching your eyes. It is unnecessary for the basic student to have to watch the eyes.

CHAPTER

EIGHT

Self Defense Techniques

The following are basic beginner self-defense techniques taught to the novice Tang Soo Do students. All the techniques are simple in principle utilizing basic skills which most adults possess. After approximately three months of practice, the beginning student is introduced to one-step punching techniques and thereafter to free sparring and ultimately free fighting practice for actual street survival. The following techniques are a few examples to practice for female, as well as male, students.

BASIC DEFENSE AGAINST HAND AROUND WAIST ATTACK.
1. Approach of attacker.

2. Actual physical attack with the hand on the waist.

3. Step with the inside right foot; inside block with the forearm.

4. After the block, sweep the right arm into a cocking position for the elbow strike.

5. Elbow strike driving through to the attacker's head.

DEFENSE AGAINST SHOULDER GRAB

1. All encounters with strangers should be kept at arm's length.

2. Attacker grabs.

3. Instant reaction. Locking suspect's arm while stepping back.

4. While holding the arms in a locked position, drive the knee into the attacker's groin.

STOPPING AN ATTACK BEFORE IT STARTS.

1. Again, if possible, keep suspicious people at arm's length.

2. Attacker moves towards defender.

3. Thrusting palm strike to the face stopping the attacker.

4. Clawing face, grasping eye-sockets. Discretion is used on how much force is employed to stop the attack.

ATTACK FROM REAR.

1. Attacker grabs defender by the shoulder from the rear. First reaction is to look and identify the suspect.

2. Stepping toward the attacker utilizing a outside block and cocking the right hand for a reverse punch.

3. Option to strike or not.

ATTACK FROM REAR
1. Attacking from rear.

2. Bear Hug Grab from the rear. Defender looks down looking for hand grasp and feet placement.

3. Bumping backwards with the hips to distract the attacker.

4. Cocking the right leg up instantly.

5. Stomping with the heel — driving with the heel into the attacker's instep.

6. Breaking the Bear Hug upwards as the attacker is recovering from the heel smash.

7. Cocking elbow after the break-away upwards.

8. Swinging downwards to the rear with a hammerfist strike to the groin.

FRONT CHOKE BREAK-AWAY

1. Attacker approaches from the front.

2. Two hand choke to the neck.

3. Instantly drawing the right hand to the side, the left hand is raised high.

4. Stepping to the rear, driving the left arm downwards and across breaking the hold from the neck.

5. After the break-away, striking the attacker with a back knuckle strike to the temple.

FRESH GUY DEFENSE
Six Steps to Give an Unwanted Fresh Guy a Message.
1. Approached from the rear.

2. Subject places his arm around the shoulders.

3. Stepping forward with the leg closest to the subject, cocking the elbow upwards.

4. Driving the elbow into the subject's mid-section.

5. Stepping across and pivoting around breaking the subject's arm around the shoulders.

6. Complete break, facing subject.

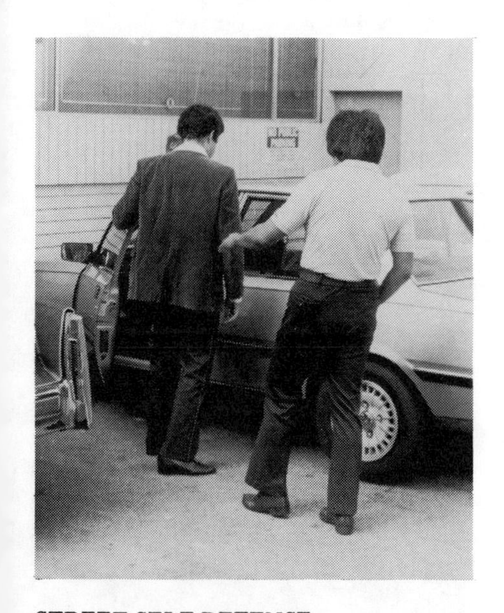

STREET SELF DEFENSE

1. Attackers approach victim at his vehicle.

2. First one grabs victim.

3. Victim reacts with a block and a reverse punch.

4. Before the attacker recovers, he is grabbed by the victim.

5. Knee to the chest.

6. Elbow to the neck.

DEFENSE AGAINST A GUN I

1. Hold-up situation in the parking lot.

2. Split-second reaction, pivot the body inside (out of the line of fire.

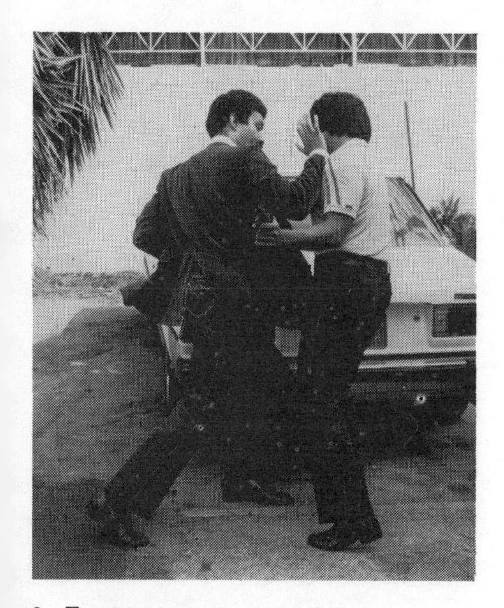

3. Forehand smash to the face.

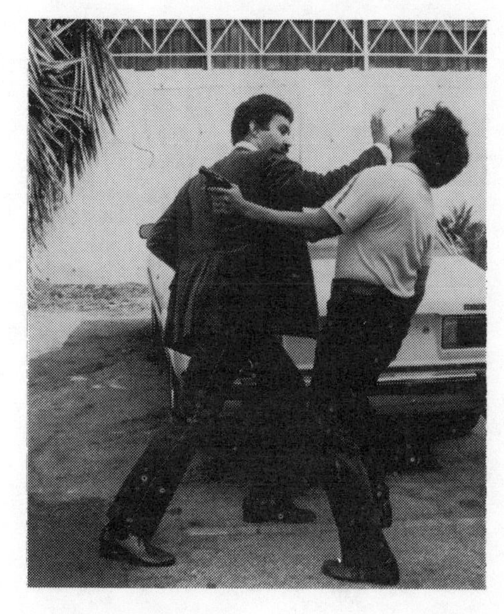

4. Driving through.

5. Follow-up with a knee to the groin.

DEFENSE AGAINST A GUN II

1. Cooperate with the robber's demands.

2. Reflex. Pivot out of the line of fire.

3. Grab the gun as you block, pulling the gun forward and downwards.

4. Swing the gun up and over away from the body into a wrist lock. (Keep the robber off balance.)

5. Pull the gun out of the robber's hand.

6. Reverse the role.

DEFENSE AGAINST A KNIFE ATTACK
1. Relax and be passive.

2. Grab the hand holding the knife. (Even if you have to get cut, it is better than being stabbed.)

3. Use the elbow because you are in close quarters.

4. Separate the knife from the thug.

5. Follow-up after you gain the edge over the robber.